The
Poetry of
Alfred,
Lord
Tennyson

The Poetry of Alfred, Lord Tennyson

This edition published in 2020 by Arcturus Publishing Limited
26/27 Bickels Yard, 151–153 Bermondsey Street,
London SE1 3HA

Copyright © Arcturus Holdings Limited

All rights reserved. No part of this publication may be reproduced, stored in a retrieval system, or transmitted, in any form or by any means, electronic, mechanical, photocopying, recording or otherwise, without prior written permission in accordance with the provisions of the Copyright Act 1956 (as amended). Any person or persons who do any unauthorised act in relation to this publication may be liable to criminal prosecution and civil claims for damages.

AD007495UK

Printed in the UK

Contents

Introduction	7
Œnone	9
Timbuctoo	19
The Mermaid	28
Recollections of the Arabian Nights	30
The Kraken	36
Claribel	37
Mariana	38
A Dream of Fair Women	41
The Palace of Art	53
Mariana in the South	65
The Lotos Eaters	69
Choric Song	71
St Simeon Stylites	76
Ulysses	84
The Two Voices	87
Morte d'Arthur	107
Break, Break, Break	117
St Agnes' Eve	118
Locksley Hall	120
The Lady of Shalott (1842 revision)	134
Godiva	141
The Vision of Sin	144
Lady Clara Vere de Vere	153
Tears, Idle Tears (from *The Princess*)	156
Ask Me No More (from *The Princess*)	157
Ring Out, Wild Bells (from *In Memoriam*)	158
I Envy Not in Any Moods (from *In Memoriam*)	160

The Eagle	161
Ode on the Death of the Duke of Wellington	162
The Charge of the Light Brigade	172
Come into the Garden, Maud (from *Maud*)	175
The War	178
Tithonus	179
Song from the Marriage of Geraint (from *Idylls of the King*)	182
In the Valley of Cauteretz	183
Northern Farmer (Old Style)	184
Northern Farmer (New Style)	188
Lucretius	192
Marriage Morning	202
Tiresias	203
The Ancient Sage	209
Crossing the Bar	219
Index of First Lines	221

Introduction

Born in 1809, in Somersby in rural Lincolnshire, England, Alfred was the fourth of twelve children of the Reverend George Tennyson and his wife Elizabeth. Despite the veneer of middle-class respectability, the family's home life was not a happy one. Disinherited by his father, George became depressed and embittered, taking out his anger on the family during drunken rages. The shy, young Alfred sought refuge in poetry, continuing to write while at grammar school. In 1827 he went to the University of Cambridge, publishing a collection of poems with his brothers, Frederick and Charles, in the same year. His first solo collection, *Poems, Chiefly Lyrical*, followed three years later, but soon after a series of tragedies struck.

First, in 1831, his father died, plunging the family into debt and forcing Alfred to leave Cambridge. In an attempt to make money, he published another collection, *Poems*, in 1832. Despite containing early drafts of some of his greatest poems, such as 'The Lady of Shalott' and 'Mariana in the South', the collection was savaged by critics. The most scathing comments came from John Wilson Croker, whose review of 'Edymion', Shelley and Byron claimed, killed Keats. Though the criticism discouraged him, it was the death of Arthur Hallam, his closest friend and his sisters' fiancé, that left him devastated. He resolved never to publish poetry again.

He did not stop writing, however. On the contrary, the emotions he felt during the following years led to an outpouring of poems, including 'Ulysses', 'Morte d'Arthur' and 'Break, Break, Break'. After nine years he finally resolved to publish his work once more. *Poems*, published in two volumes in 1842, contained new writing and revised editions of earlier works. It was enthusiastically received and his reputation soared.

In 1850 he published *In Memoriam*, an elegy and requiem for his friend Arthur Hallam. It was a huge success with both critics and the public alike. The poem and its success helped gain him his appointment as Poet Laureate later that year after the death of William Wordsworth. One of its most famous readers was Queen Victoria, who turned to the book after the death of her husband Prince Albert. She would later state: 'Next to the Bible, *In Memoriam* is my comfort.'

The same year also brought him romantic fulfilment. After a ten-year engagement, he finally married Emily Sellwood. The couple had two sons, Hallam and Lionel. They lived for some time in Farringford House on the Isle of Wight, before the unwanted attention of adoring fans drove them to seek a more solitary home in Aldworth in West Sussex. Though Tennyson guarded his privacy, he also enthusiastically engaged in the public side of his role as Poet Laureate, publishing patriotic pieces such as 'The Charge of the Light Brigade' and 'Ode on the Death of the Duke of Wellington'. His popularity continued to grow and in 1864 he released his bestselling collection, *Enoch Arden and Other Poems*, which sold more than 40,000 copies.

He spared nothing in his efforts to be the 'people's poet', writing works of varying length, form, metre, style and rhyming scheme. He continually revised and republished new versions of old poems and even tried his hand at drama. In 1883, he accepted a peerage, becoming the first Baron Tennyson. He died at his home in Aldworth, Sussex, on 6 October 1892 and was buried the following week in Poets' Corner at Westminster Abbey.

Œnone

There lies a vale in Ida, lovelier
Than all the valleys of Ionian hills.
The swimming vapour slopes athwart the glen,
Puts forth an arm, and creeps from pine to pine,
And loiters, slowly drawn. On either hand
The lawns and meadow-ledges midway down
Hang rich in flowers, and far below them roars
The long brook falling thro' the clov'n ravine
In cataract after cataract to the sea.
Behind the valley topmost Gargarus
Stands up and takes the morning: but in front
The gorges, opening wide apart, reveal
Troas and Ilion's column'd citadel,
The crown of Troas.

                Hither came at noon
Mournful Œnone, wandering forlorn
Of Paris, once her playmate on the hills.
Her cheek had lost the rose, and round her neck
Floated her hair or seem'd to float in rest.
She, leaning on a fragment twined with vine,
Sang to the stillness, till the mountain-shade
Sloped downward to her seat from the upper cliff.

'O mother Ida, many-fountain'd Ida,
Dear mother Ida, harken ere I die.
For now the noonday quiet holds the hill:
The grasshopper is silent in the grass:
The lizard, with his shadow on the stone,
Rests like a shadow, and the winds are dead.
The purple flower droops: the golden bee

Is lily-cradled: I alone awake.
My eyes are full of tears, my heart of love,
My heart is breaking, and my eyes are dim,
And I am all aweary of my life.

    'O mother Ida, many-fountain'd Ida,
Dear mother Ida, harken ere I die.
Hear me, O Earth, hear me, O Hills, O Caves
That house the cold crown'd snake! O mountain brooks,
I am the daughter of a River-God,
Hear me, for I will speak, and build up all
My sorrow with my song, as yonder walls
Rose slowly to a music slowly breathed,
A cloud that gather'd shape: for it may be
That, while I speak of it, a little while
My heart may wander from its deeper woe.

    'O mother Ida, many-fountain'd Ida,
Dear mother Ida, harken ere I die.
I waited underneath the dawning hills,
Aloft the mountain lawn was dewy-dark,
And dewy-dark aloft the mountain pine:
Beautiful Paris, evil-hearted Paris,
Leading a jet-black goat white-horn'd, white-hooved,
Came up from reedy Simois all alone.

    'O mother Ida, harken ere I die.
Far-off the torrent call'd me from the cleft:
Far up the solitary morning smote
The streaks of virgin snow. With down-dropt eyes
I sat alone: white-breasted like a star
Fronting the dawn he moved; a leopard skin

Droop'd from his shoulder, but his sunny hair
Cluster'd about his temples like a God's:
And his cheek brighten'd as the foam-bow brightens
When the wind blows the foam, and all my heart
Went forth to embrace him coming ere he came.

   'Dear mother Ida, harken ere I die.
He smiled, and opening out his milk-white palm
Disclosed a fruit of pure Hesperian gold,
That smelt ambrosially, and while I look'd
And listen'd, the full-flowing river of speech
Came down upon my heart.
                        '"My own Œnone,
Beautiful-brow'd Œnone, my own soul,
Behold this fruit, whose gleaming rind ingrav'n
'For the most fair,' would seem to award it thine,
As lovelier than whatever Oread haunt
The knolls of Ida, loveliest in all grace
Of movement, and the charm of married brows."

   'Dear mother Ida, harken ere I die.
He prest the blossom of his lips to mine,
And added 'This was cast upon the board,
When all the full-faced presence of the Gods
Ranged in the halls of Peleus; whereupon
Rose feud, with question unto whom 'twere due:
But light-foot Iris brought it yester-eve,
Delivering that to me, by common voice
Elected umpire, Herè comes to-day,
Pallas and Aphroditè, claiming each
This meed of fairest. Thou, within the cave
Behind yon whispering tuft of oldest pine,

Mayst well behold them unbeheld, unheard
Hear all, and see thy Paris judge of Gods.'

'Dear mother Ida, harken ere I die.
It was the deep midnoon: one silvery cloud
Had lost his way between the piney sides
Of this long glen. Then to the bower they came,
Naked they came to that smooth-swarded bower,
And at their feet the crocus brake like fire,
Violet, amaracus, and asphodel,
Lotos and lilies: and a wind arose,
And overhead the wandering ivy and vine,
This way and that, in many a wild festoon
Ran riot, garlanding the gnarled boughs
With bunch and berry and flower thro' and thro'.

'O mother Ida, harken ere I die.
On the tree-tops a crested peacock lit,
And o'er him flow'd a golden cloud, and lean'd
Upon him, slowly dropping fragrant dew.
Then first I heard the voice of her, to whom
Coming thro' Heaven, like a light that grows
Larger and clearer, with one mind the Gods
Rise up for reverence. She to Paris made
Proffer of royal power, ample rule
Unquestion'd, overflowing revenue
Wherewith to embellish state, "from many a vale
And river-sunder'd champaign clothed with corn,
Or labour'd mine undrainable of ore.
Honour," she said, "and homage, tax and toll,
From many an inland town and haven large,

Mast-throng'd beneath her shadowing citadel
In glassy bays among her tallest towers."

'O mother Ida, harken ere I die.
Still she spake on and still she spake of power,
Which in all action is the end of all;
Power fitted to the season; wisdom-bred
And throned of wisdom – from all neighbour crowns
Alliance and allegiance, till thy hand
Fail from the sceptre-staff. Such boon from me,
From me, Heaven's Queen, Paris, to thee king-born,
A shepherd all thy life but yet king-born,
Should come most welcome, seeing men, in power
Only, are likest Gods, who have attain'd
Rest in a happy place and quiet seats
Above the thunder, with undying bliss
In knowledge of their own supremacy.'

'Dear mother Ida, harken ere I die.
She ceased, and Paris held the costly fruit
Out at arm's-length, so much the thought of power
Flatter'd his spirit; but Pallas where she stood
Somewhat apart, her clear and bared limbs
O'erthwarted with the brazen-headed spear
Upon her pearly shoulder leaning cold,
The while, above, her full and earnest eye
Over her snow-cold breast and angry cheek
Kept watch, waiting decision, made reply.

'"Self-reverence, self-knowledge, self-control,
These three alone lead life to sovereign power.

Yet not for power (power of herself
Would come uncall'd for) but to live by law,
Acting the law we live by without fear;
And, because right is right, to follow right
Were wisdom in the scorn of consequence."'

'Dear mother Ida, harken ere I die.
Again she said: "I woo thee not with gifts.
Sequel of guerdon could not alter me
To fairer. Judge thou me by what I am,
So shalt thou find me fairest.

                      Yet, indeed,
If gazing on divinity disrobed
Thy mortal eyes are frail to judge of fair,
Unbias'd by self-profit, oh! rest thee sure
That I shall love thee well and cleave to thee,
So that my vigour, wedded to thy blood,
Shall strike within thy pulses, like a God's,
To push thee forward thro' a life of shocks,
Dangers, and deeds, until endurance grow
Sinew'd with action, and the full-grown will,
Circled thro' all experiences, pure law,
Commeasure perfect freedom."

                      'Here she ceas'd
And Paris ponder'd, and I cried, "O Paris,
Give it to Pallas!" but he heard me not,
Or hearing would not hear me, woe is me!

'O mother Ida, many-fountain'd Ida,
Dear mother Ida, harken ere I die.
Idalian Aphroditè beautiful,

Fresh as the foam, new-bathed in Paphian wells,
With rosy slender fingers backward drew
From her warm brows and bosom her deep hair
Ambrosial, golden round her lucid throat
And shoulder: from the violets her light foot
Shone rosy-white, and o'er her rounded form
Between the shadows of the vine-bunches
Floated the glowing sunlights, as she moved.

   'Dear mother Ida, harken ere I die.
She with a subtle smile in her mild eyes,
The herald of her triumph, drawing nigh
Half-whisper'd in his ear, "I promise thee
The fairest and most loving wife in Greece,"
She spoke and laugh'd: I shut my sight for fear:
But when I look'd, Paris had raised his arm,
And I beheld great Herè's angry eyes,
As she withdrew into the golden cloud,
And I was left alone within the bower;
And from that time to this I am alone,
And I shall be alone until I die.

   'Yet, mother Ida, harken ere I die.
Fairest – why fairest wife? am I not fair?
My love hath told me so a thousand times.
Methinks I must be fair, for yesterday,
When I past by, a wild and wanton pard,
Eyed like the evening star, with playful tail
Crouch'd fawning in the weed. Most loving is she?
Ah me, my mountain shepherd, that my arms
Were wound about thee, and my hot lips prest

Close, close to thine in that quick-falling dew
Of fruitful kisses, thick as Autumn rains
Flash in the pools of whirling Simois.

   'O mother, hear me yet before I die.
They came, they cut away my tallest pines,
My tall dark pines, that plumed the craggy ledge
High over the blue gorge, and all between
The snowy peak and snow-white cataract
Foster'd the callow eaglet – from beneath
Whose thick mysterious boughs in the dark morn
The panther's roar came muffled, while I sat
Low in the valley. Never, never more
Shall lone Œnone see the morning mist
Sweep thro' them; never see them overlaid
With narrow moon-lit slips of silver cloud,
Between the loud stream and the trembling stars.

   'O mother, hear me yet before I die.
I wish that somewhere in the ruin'd folds,
Among the fragments tumbled from the glens,
Or the dry thickets, I could meet with her
The Abominable, that uninvited came
Into the fair Peleïan banquet-hall,
And cast the golden fruit upon the board,
And bred this change; that I might speak my mind,
And tell her to her face how much I hate
Her presence, hated both of Gods and men.

   'O mother, hear me yet before I die.
Hath he not sworn his love a thousand times,
In this green valley, under this green hill,

Ev'n on this hand, and sitting on this stone?
Seal'd it with kisses? water'd it with tears?
O happy tears, and how unlike to these!
O happy Heaven, how canst thou see my face?
O happy earth, how canst thou bear my weight?
O death, death, death, thou ever-floating cloud,
There are enough unhappy on this earth,
Pass by the happy souls, that love to live:
I pray thee, pass before my light of life,
And shadow all my soul, that I may die.
Thou weighest heavy on the heart within,
Weigh heavy on my eyelids: let me die.

   'O mother, hear me yet before I die.
I will not die alone, for fiery thoughts
Do shape themselves within me, more and more,
Whereof I catch the issue, as I hear
Dead sounds at night come from the inmost hills,
Like footsteps upon wool. I dimly see
My far-off doubtful purpose, as a mother
Conjectures of the features of her child
Ere it is born: her child! – a shudder comes
Across me: never child be born of me,
Unblest, to vex me with his father's eyes!

   'O mother, hear me yet before I die.
Hear me, O earth. I will not die alone,
Lest their shrill happy laughter come to me
Walking the cold and starless road of death
Uncomforted, leaving my ancient love
With the Greek woman. I will rise and go
Down into Troy, and ere the stars come forth

Talk with the wild Cassandra, for she says
A fire dances before her, and a sound
Rings ever in her ears of armed men.
What this may be I know not, but I know
That, wheresoe'er I am by night and day,
All earth and air seem only burning fire.'

Timbuctoo

Deep in the lion-haunted inland lies
A mystic city, goal of high emprise.
Chapman

I stood upon the Mountain which o'erlooks
The narrow seas, whose rapid interval
Parts Afric from green Europe, when the Sun
Had fall'n below th' Atlantic, and above
The silent heavens were blench'd with faëry light,
Uncertain whether faëry light or cloud,
Flowing Southward, and the chasms of deep, deep blue
Slumber'd unfathomable, and the stars
Were flooded over with clear glory and pale.
I gazed upon the sheeny coast beyond,
There where the Giant of old Time infix'd
The limits of his prowess, pillars high
Long time erased from Earth: even as the Sea
When weary of wild inroad buildeth up
Huge mounds whereby to stay his yeasty waves.
And much I mused on legends quaint and old
Which whilom won the hearts of all on earth
Toward their brightness, ev'n as flame draws air;
But had their being in the heart of man
As air is th' life of flame: and thou wert then
A centr'd glory-circled memory,
Divinest Atalantis, whom the waves
Have buried deep, and thou of later name,
Imperial Eldorado, roof'd with gold:
Shadows to which, despite all shocks of change,
All on-set of capricious accident,

Men clung with yearning Hope which would not die.
As when in some great City where the walls
Shake, and the streets with ghastly faces throng'd,
Do utter forth a subterranean voice,
Among the inner columns far retired
At midnight, in the lone Acropolis,
Before the awful Genius of the place
Kneels the pale Priestess in deep faith, the while
Above her head the weak lamp dips and winks
Unto the fearful summoning without:
Nathless she ever clasps the marble knees,
Bathes the cold hand with tears, and gazeth on
Those eyes which wear no light but that wherewith
Her phantasy informs them.
                      Where are ye,
Thrones of the Western wave, fair Islands green?
Where are your moonlight halls, your cedarn glooms,
The blossoming abysses of your hills?
Your flowering Capes and your gold-sanded bays
Blown round with happy airs of odorous winds?
Where are the infinite ways which, Seraph-trod,
Wound thro' your great Elysian solitudes,
Whose lowest depths were, as with visible love,
Fill'd with Divine effulgence, circumfused,
Flowing between the clear and polish'd stems,
And ever circling round their emerald cones
In coronals and glories, such as gird
The unfading foreheads of the Saints in Heaven?
For nothing visible, they say, had birth
In that blest ground but it was play'd about
With its peculiar glory. Then I raised
My voice and cried, 'Wide Afric, doth thy Sun

Lighten, thy hills enfold a city as fair
As those which starr'd the night o' the elder world?
Or is the rumour of thy Timbuctoo
A dream as frail as those of ancient Time?'

    A curve of whitening, flashing, ebbing light!
A rustling of white wings! the bright descent
Of a young Seraph! and he stood beside me
There on the ridge, and look'd into my face
With his unutterable, shining orbs,
So that with hasty motion I did veil
My vision with both hands, and saw before me
Such colour'd spots as dance athwart the eyes
Of those that gaze upon the noonday Sun.
Girt with a zone of flashing gold beneath
His breast, and compass'd round about his brow
With triple arch of everchanging bows,
And circled with the glory of living light
And alternation of all hues, he stood.

    'O child of man, why muse you here alone
Upon the Mountain, on the dreams of old
Which fill'd the earth with passing loveliness,
Which flung strange music on the howling winds,
And odours rapt from remote Paradise?
Thy sense is clogged with dull mortality;
Thy spirit fetter'd with the bond of clay:
Open thine eyes and see.'

                      I look'd, but not
Upon his face, for it was wonderful
With its exceeding brightness, and the light
Of the great Angel Mind which look'd from out
The starry glowing of his restless eyes.
I felt my soul grow mighty, and my spirit

With supernatural excitation bound
Within me, and my mental eye grew large
With such a vast circumference of thought,
That in my vanity I seem'd to stand
Upon the outward verge and bound alone
Of full beatitude. Each failing sense
As with a momentary flash of light,
Grew thrillingly distinct and keen. I saw
The smallest grain that dappled the dark earth,
The indistinctest atom in deep air,
The Moon's white cities, and the opal width
Of her small glowing lakes, her silver heights
Unvisited with dew of vagrant cloud,
And the unsounded, undescended depth
Of her black hollows. The clear Galaxy
Shorn of its hoary lustre, wonderful,
Distinct and vivid with sharp points of light,
Blaze within blaze, an unimagin'd depth
And harmony of planet-girded suns
And moon-encircled planets, wheel in wheel,
Arch'd the wan sapphire. Nay — the hum of men,
Or other things talking in unknown tongues,
And notes of busy life in distant worlds
Beat like a far wave on my anxious ear.

    A maze of piercing, trackless, thrilling thoughts
Involving and embracing each with each,
Rapid as fire, inextricably link'd,
Expanding momently with every sight
And sound which struck the palpitating sense,
The issue of strong impulse, hurried through
The riv'n rapt brain; as when in some large lake
From pressure of descendant crags, which lapse

Disjointed, crumbling from their parent slope
At slender interval, the level calm
Is ridg'd with restless and increasing spheres
Which break upon each other, each th' effect
Of separate impulse, but more fleet and strong
Than its precursor, till the eyes in vain
Amid the wild unrest of swimming shade
Dappled with hollow and alternate rise
Of interpenetrated arc, would scan
Definite round.
                  I know not if I shape
These things with accurate similitude
From visible objects, for but dimly now,
Less vivid than a half-forgotten dream,
The memory of that mental excellence
Comes o'er me, and it may be I entwine
The indecision of my present mind
With its past clearness, yet it seems to me
As even then the torrent of quick thought
Absorbed me from the nature of itself
With its own fleetness. Where is he that, borne
Adown the sloping of an arrowy stream,
Could link his shallop to the fleeting edge,
And muse midway with philosophic calm
Upon the wondrous laws which regulate
The fierceness of the bounding Element?
    My thoughts which long had grovell'd in the slime
Of this dull world, like dusky worms which house
Beneath unshaken waters, but at once
Upon some Earth-awakening day of Spring
Do pass from gloom to glory, and aloft
Winnow the purple, bearing on both sides

Double display of star-lit wings, which burn
Fan-like and fibred, with intensest bloom;
Ev'n so my thoughts, erewhile so low, now felt
Unutterable buoyancy and strength
To bear them upward through the trackless fields
Of undefin'd existence far and free.

      Then first within the South methought I saw
A wilderness of spires, and chrystal pile
Of rampart upon rampart, dome on dome,
Illimitable range of battlement
On battlement, and the Imperial height
Of Canopy o'ercanopied.

                    Behind
In diamond light upspring the dazzling peaks
Of Pyramids, as far surpassing earth's
As heaven than earth is fairer. Each aloft
Upon his narrowed eminence bore globes
Of wheeling Suns, or Stars, or semblances
Of either, showering circular abyss
Of radiance. But the glory of the place
Stood out a pillared front of burnish'd gold,
Interminably high, if gold it were
Or metal more ethereal, and beneath
Two doors of blinding brilliance, where no gaze
Might rest, stood open, and the eye could scan,
Through length of porch and valve and boundless hall,
Part of a throne of fiery flame, wherefrom
The snowy skirting of a garment hung,
And glimpse of multitude of multitudes
That ministered around it – if I saw
These things distinctly, for my human brain
Stagger'd beneath the vision, and thick night

Came down upon my eyelids, and I fell.

    With ministering hand he rais'd me up:
Then with a mournful and ineffable smile,
Which but to look on for a moment filled
My eyes with irresistible sweet tears,
In accents of majestic melody,
Like a swoln river's gushings in still night
Mingled with floating music, thus he spake:

    'There is no mightier Spirit than I to sway
The heart of man; and teach him to attain
By shadowing forth the Unattainable;
And step by step to scale that mighty stair
Whose landing-place is wrapt about with clouds
Of glory' of heaven. With earliest light of Spring,
And in the glow of sallow Summertide,
And in red Autumn when the winds are wild
With gambols, and when full-voiced Winter roofs
The headland with inviolate white snow,
I play about his heart a thousand ways,
Visit his eyes with visions, and his ears
With harmonies of wind and wave and wood,
– Of winds which tell of waters, and of waters
Betraying the close kisses of the wind –
And win him unto me: and few there be
So gross of heart who have not felt and known
A higher than they see: They with dim eyes
Behold me darkling. Lo! I have given thee
To understand my presence, and to feel
My fullness; I have fill'd thy lips with power.
I have rais'd thee higher to the spheres of Heaven,
Man's first, last home: and thou with ravish'd sense
Listenest the lordly music flowing from

Th' illimitable years. I am the Spirit,
The permeating life which courseth through
All th' intricate and labyrinthine veins
Of the great vine of Fable, which, outspread
With growth of shadowing leaf and clusters rare,
Reacheth to every corner under Heaven,
Deep-rooted in the living soil of truth;
So that men's hopes and fears take refuge in
The fragrance of its complicated glooms,
And cool impeachèd twilights. Child of Man,
See'st thou yon river, whose translucent wave,
Forth issuing from the darkness, windeth through
The argent streets o' th' City, imaging
The soft inversion of her tremulous Domes,
Her gardens frequent with the stately Palm,
Her Pagods hung with music of sweet bells,
Her obelisks of rangèd chrysolite,
Minarets and towers? Lo! how he passeth by,
And gulphs himself in sands, as not enduring
To carry through the world those waves, which bore
The reflex of my City in their depth.
Oh City! oh latest Throne! where I was rais'd
To be a mystery of loveliness
Unto all eyes, the time is well-nigh come
When I must render up this glorious home
To keen Discovery; soon yon brilliant towers
Shall darken with the waving of her wand;
Darken and shrink and shiver into huts,
Black specks amid a waste of dreary sand,
Low-built, mud-walled, barbarian settlements.
How changed from this fair city!'
                                    Thus far the Spirit:

Then parted Heaven-ward on the wing: and I
Was left alone on Calpe, and the Moon
Had fallen from the night, and all was dark!

The Mermaid

I

Who would be
A mermaid fair,
Singing alone,
Combing her hair
Under the sea,
In a golden curl
With a comb of pearl,
On a throne?

II

I would be a mermaid fair;
I would sing to myself the whole of the day;
With a comb of pearl I would comb my hair;
And still as I comb'd I would sing and say
'Who is it loves me? who loves not me?'
I would comb my hair till my ringlets would fall,
    Low adown, low adown,
From under my starry sea-bud crown
    Low adown and around,
And I should look like a fountain of gold
    Springing alone
  With a shrill inner sound,
    Over the throne
  In the midst of the hall;
Till that great sea-snake under the sea
From his coiled sleeps in the central deeps
Would slowly trail himself sevenfold
Round the hall where I sate, and look in at the gate
With his large calm eyes for the love of me.

And all the mermen under the sea
Would feel their immortality
Die in their hands for the love of me.

III

But at night I would wander away, away,
   I would fling on each side my low-flowing locks,
And lightly vault from the throne and play
   With the mermen in and out of the rocks;
We would run to and fro, and hide and seek,
   On the broad sea-wolds in the crimson shells,
   Whose silvery spikes are nighest the sea.
But if any came near I would call, and shriek,
And adown the steep like a wave I would leap
   From the diamond-ledges that jut from the dells;
For I would not be kiss'd by all who would list,
   Of the bold merry mermen under the sea;
   They would sue me, and woo me, and flatter me,
   In the purple twilights under the sea;
   But the king of them all would carry me,
   Woo me, and win me, and marry me,
   In the branching jaspers under the sea;
Then all the dry pied things that be
   In the hueless mosses under the sea
Would curl round my silver feet silently,
All looking up for the love of me.
And if I should carol aloud, from aloft
All things that are forked, and horned, and soft
Would lean out from the hollow sphere of the sea,
All looking down for the love of me.

Recollections of the Arabian Nights

When the breeze of a joyful dawn blew free
In the silken sail of infancy,
The tide of time flow'd back with me,
    The forward-flowing tide of time;
And many a sheeny summer-morn,
Adown the Tigris I was borne,
By Bagdat's shrines of fretted gold,
High-walled gardens green and old;
True Mussulman was I and sworn,
  For it was in the golden prime
      Of good Haroun Alraschid.

Anight my shallop, rustling thro'
The low and bloomed foliage, drove
The fragrant, glistening deeps, and clove
The citron-shadows in the blue:
By garden porches on the brim,
The costly doors flung open wide,
Gold glittering thro' lamplight dim,
And broider'd sofas on each side:
  In sooth it was a goodly time,
  For it was in the golden prime
      Of good Haroun Alraschid.

Often, where clear-stemm'd platans guard
The outlet, did I turn away
The boat-head down a broad canal
From the main river sluiced, where all
The sloping of the moon-lit sward
Was damask-work, and deep inlay

Of braided blooms unmown, which crept
Adown to where the water slept.
   A goodly place, a goodly time,
    For it was in the golden prime
       Of good Haroun Alraschid.

A motion from the river won
Ridged the smooth level, bearing on
My shallop thro' the star-strown calm,
Until another night in night
I enter'd, from the clearer light,
Imbower'd vaults of pillar'd palm,
Imprisoning sweets, which, as they clomb
Heavenward, were stay'd beneath the dome
   Of hollow boughs. – A goodly time,
    For it was in the golden prime
       Of good Haroun Alraschid.

Still onward; and the clear canal
Is rounded to as clear a lake.
From the green rivage many a fall
Of diamond rillets musical,
Thro' little crystal arches low
Down from the central fountain's flow
Fall'n silver-chiming, seem'd to shake
The sparkling flints beneath the prow.
   A goodly place, a goodly time,
    For it was in the golden prime
       Of good Haroun Alraschid.

Above thro' many a bowery turn
A walk with vary-colour'd shells

Wander'd engrain'd. On either side
All round about the fragrant marge
From fluted vase, and brazen urn
In order, eastern flowers large,
Some dropping low their crimson bells
Half-closed, and others studded wide
   With disks and tiars, fed the time
   With odour in the golden prime
      Of good Haroun Alraschid.

Far off, and where the lemon grove
In closest coverture upsprung,
The living airs of middle night
Died round the bulbul as he sung;
Not he: but something which possess'd
The darkness of the world, delight,
Life, anguish, death, immortal love,
Ceasing not, mingled, unrepress'd,
   Apart from place, withholding time,
   But flattering the golden prime
      Of good Haroun Alraschid.

Black the garden-bowers and grots
Slumber'd: the solemn palms were ranged
Above, unwoo'd of summer wind:
A sudden splendour from behind
Flush'd all the leaves with rich gold-green,
And, flowing rapidly between
Their interspaces, counterchanged
The level lake with diamond-plots

Of dark and bright. A lovely time,
For it was in the golden prime
    Of good Haroun Alraschid.

Dark-blue the deep sphere overhead,
Distinct with vivid stars inlaid,
Grew darker from that under-flame:
So, leaping lightly from the boat,
With silver anchor left afloat,
In marvel whence that glory came
Upon me, as in sleep I sank
In cool soft turf upon the bank,
  Entranced with that place and time,
  So worthy of the golden prime
    Of good Haroun Alraschid.

Thence thro' the garden I was drawn –
A realm of pleasance, many a mound,
And many a shadow-chequer'd lawn
Full of the city's stilly sound,
And deep myrrh-thickets blowing round
The stately cedar, tamarisks,
Thick rosaries of scented thorn,
Tall orient shrubs, and obelisks
  Graven with emblems of the time,
  In honour of the golden prime
    Of good Haroun Alraschid.

With dazed vision unawares
From the long alley's latticed shade
Emerged, I came upon the great
Pavilion of the Caliphat.

Right to the carven cedarn doors,
Flung inward over spangled floors,
Broad-based flights of marble stairs
Ran up with golden balustrade,
   After the fashion of the time,
    And humour of the golden prime
      Of good Haroun Alraschid.

The fourscore windows all alight
As with the quintessence of flame,
A million tapers flaring bright
From twisted silvers look'd to shame
The hollow-vaulted dark, and stream'd
Upon the mooned domes aloof
In inmost Bagdat, till there seem'd
Hundreds of crescents on the roof
   Of night new-risen, that marvellous time,
    To celebrate the golden prime
      Of good Haroun Alraschid.

Then stole I up, and trancedly
Gazed on the Persian girl alone,
Serene with argent-lidded eyes
Amorous, and lashes like to rays
Of darkness, and a brow of pearl
Tressed with redolent ebony,
In many a dark delicious curl,
Flowing beneath her rose-hued zone;
   The sweetest lady of the time,
    Well worthy of the golden prime
      Of good Haroun Alraschid.

Six columns, three on either side,
Pure silver, underpropt a rich
Throne of the massive ore, from which
Down-droop'd, in many a floating fold,
Engarlanded and diaper'd
With inwrought flowers, a cloth of gold.
Thereon, his deep eye laughter-stirr'd
With merriment of kingly pride,
    Sole star of all that place and time,
    I saw him – in his golden prime,
        The Good Haroun Alraschid!

The Kraken

Below the thunders of the upper deep;
Far, far beneath in the abysmal sea,
His ancient, dreamless, uninvaded sleep
The Kraken sleepeth: faintest sunlights flee
About his shadowy sides: above him swell
Huge sponges of millennial growth and height;
And far away into the sickly light,
From many a wondrous grot and secret cell
Unnumber'd and enormous polypi
Winnow with giant arms the slumbering green.
There hath he lain for ages, and will lie
Battening upon huge seaworms in his sleep,
Until the latter fire shall heat the deep;
Then once by man and angels to be seen,
In roaring he shall rise and on the surface die.

Claribel

A Melody

I

Where Claribel low-lieth
    The breezes pause and die,
Letting the rose-leaves fall:
    But the solemn oak-tree sigheth,
        Thick-leaved, ambrosial,
    With an ancient melody
    Of an inward agony,
Where Claribel low-lieth.

II

At eve the beetle boometh
    Athwart the thicket lone:
At noon the wild bee hummeth
    About the moss'd headstone:
At midnight the moon cometh,
    And looketh down alone.
Her song the lintwhite swelleth,
The clear-voiced mavis dwelleth,
    The callow throstle lispeth,
The slumbrous wave outwelleth,
    The babbling runnel crispeth,
The hollow grot replieth
    Where Claribel low-lieth.

Mariana

With blackest moss the flower-plots
    Were thickly crusted, one and all:
The rusted nails fell from the knots
    That held the pear to the gable-wall.
The broken sheds look'd sad and strange:
    Unlifted was the clinking latch;
    Weeded and worn the ancient thatch
Upon the lonely moated grange.
        She only said, 'My life is dreary,
            He cometh not,' she said;
        She said, 'I am aweary, aweary,
            I would that I were dead!'

Her tears fell with the dews at even;
    Her tears fell ere the dews were dried;
She could not look on the sweet heaven,
    Either at morn or eventide.
After the flitting of the bats,
    When thickest dark did trance the sky,
    She drew her casement-curtain by,
And glanced athwart the glooming flats.
        She only said, 'The night is dreary,
            He cometh not,' she said;
        She said, 'I am aweary, aweary,
            I would that I were dead!'

Upon the middle of the night,
    Waking she heard the night-fowl crow:
The cock sung out an hour ere light:
    From the dark fen the oxen's low

Came to her: without hope of change,
    In sleep she seem'd to walk forlorn,
    Till cold winds woke the gray-eyed
        morn
About the lonely moated grange.
        She only said, 'The day is dreary,
            He cometh not,' she said;
        She said, 'I am aweary, aweary,
            I would that I were dead!'

About a stone-cast from the wall
    A sluice with blacken'd waters slept,
And o'er it many, round and small,
    The cluster'd marish-mosses crept.
Hard by a poplar shook alway,
    All silver-green with gnarled bark:
    For leagues no other tree did mark
The level waste, the rounding gray.
        She only said, 'My life is dreary,
            He cometh not,' she said;
        She said, 'I am aweary, aweary,
            I would that I were dead!'

And ever when the moon was low,
    And the shrill winds were up and
        away,
In the white curtain, to and fro,
    She saw the gusty shadow sway.
But when the moon was very low,
    And wild winds bound within their
        cell,
    The shadow of the poplar fell

Upon her bed, across her brow.
> She only said, 'The night is dreary,
> > He cometh not,' she said;
> She said, 'I am aweary, aweary,
> > I would that I were dead!'

All day within the dreamy house,
> The doors upon their hinges creak'd;
The blue fly sung in the pane; the mouse
> Behind the mouldering wainscot shriek'd,
Or from the crevice peer'd about.
> Old faces glimmer'd thro' the doors,
> Old footsteps trod the upper floors,
Old voices call'd her from without.
> She only said, 'My life is dreary,
> > He cometh not,' she said;
> She said, 'I am aweary, aweary,
> > I would that I were dead!'

The sparrow's chirrup on the roof,
> The slow clock ticking, and the sound
Which to the wooing wind aloof
> The poplar made, did all confound
Her sense; but most she loathed the hour
> When the thick-moted sunbeam lay
> Athwart the chambers, and the day
Was sloping toward his western bower.
> Then, said she, 'I am very dreary,
> > He will not come,' she said;
> She wept, 'I am aweary, aweary,
> > O God, that I were dead!'

A Dream of Fair Women

I read, before my eyelids dropt their shade,
    'The Legend of Good Women', long ago
Sung by the morning star of song, who made
    His music heard below;

Dan Chaucer, the first warbler, whose sweet breath
    Preluded those melodious bursts, that fill
The spacious times of great Elizabeth
    With sounds that echo still.

And, for a while, the knowledge of his art
    Held me above the subject, as strong gales
Hold swollen clouds from raining, tho' my heart,
    Brimful of those wild tales,

Charged both mine eyes with tears. In every land
    I saw, wherever light illumineth,
Beauty and anguish walking hand in hand
    The downward slope to death.

Those far-renowned brides of ancient song
    Peopled the hollow dark, like burning stars.
And I heard sounds of insult, shame, and wrong,
    And trumpets blown for wars;

And clattering flints batter'd with clanging hoofs:
    And I saw crowds in column'd sanctuaries;
And forms that pass'd at windows and on roofs
    Of marble palaces;

Corpses across the threshold; heroes tall
    Dislodging pinnacle and parapet
Upon the tortoise creeping to the wall;
    Lances in ambush set;

And high shrine-doors burst thro' with heated blasts.
    That run before the fluttering tongues of fire;
White surf wind-scatter'd over sails and masts,
    And ever climbing higher;

Squadrons and squares of men in brazen plates,
    Scaffolds, still sheets of water, divers woes,
Ranges of glimmering vaults with iron grates.
    And hush'd seraglios.

So shape chased shape as swift as, when to land
    Bluster the winds and tides the self-same way.
Crisp foam-flakes scud along the level sand,
    Torn from the fringe of spray.

I started once, or seem'd to start in pain.
    Resolved on noble things, and strove to speak.
As when a great thought strikes along the brain,
    And flushes all the cheek.

And once my arm was lifted to hew down
    A cavalier from off his saddle-bow.
That bore a lady from a leaguer'd town;
    And then, I know not how,

All those sharp fancies, by down-lapsing thought
    Stream'd onward, lost their edges, and did creep

Roll'd on each other, rounded, smooth'd, and brought
    Into the gulfs of sleep.

At last methought that I had wander'd far
    In an old wood: fresh-wash'd in coolest dew,
The maiden splendours of the morning star
    Shook in the steadfast blue.

Enormous elm-tree boles did stoop and lean
    Upon the dusky brushwood underneath
Their broad curved branches, fledged with clearest green,
    New from its silken sheath.

The dim red morn had died, her journey done.
    And with dead lips smiled at the twilight plain,
Half-fall'n across the threshold of the sun,
    Never to rise again.

There was no motion in the dumb dead air,
    Not any song of bird or sound of rill;
Gross darkness of the inner sepulchre
    Is not so deadly still

As that wide forest. Growths of jasmine turn'd
    Their humid arms festooning tree to tree,
And at the root thro' lush green grasses burn'd
    The red anemone.

I knew the flowers, I knew the leaves, I knew
    The tearful glimmer of the languid dawn
On those long, rank, dark wood-walks drench'd in dew,
    Leading from lawn to lawn.

The smell of violets, hidden in the green,
　　Pour'd back into my empty soul and frame
The times when I remember to have been
　　Joyful and free from blame.

And from within me a clear under-tone
　　Thrill'd thro' mine ears in that unblissful clime,
'Pass freely thro': the wood is all thine own.
　　Until the end of time.'

At length I saw a lady within call,
　　Stiller than chisell'd marble, standing there;
A daughter of the gods, divinely tall,
　　And most divinely fair.

Her loveliness with shame and with surprise
　　Froze my swift speech: she turning on my face
The star-like sorrows of immortal eyes.
　　Spoke slowly in her place.

'I had great beauty: ask thou not my name:
　　No one can be more wise than destiny.
Many drew swords and died. Where'er I came
　　I brought calamity.'

'No marvel, sovereign lady: in fair field
　　Myself for such a face had boldly died,'
I answer'd free; and turning I appeal'd
　　To one that stood beside.

But she, with sick and scornful looks averse,
　　To her full height her stately stature draws;

'My youth,' she said, 'was blasted with a curse:
    This woman was the cause.

'I was cut off from hope in that sad place,
    Which yet to name my spirit loathes and fears:
My father held his hand upon his face;
    I, blinded with my tears,

'Still strove to speak: my voice was thick with sighs
    As in a dream. Dimly I could descry
The stern black-bearded kings with wolfish eyes.
    Waiting to see me die.

'The high masts flickered as they lay afloat;
    The crowds, the temples, waver'd, and the shore;
The bright death quiver'd at the victim's throat;
    Touch'd; and I knew no more.'

Whereto the other with a downward brow:
    'I would the white cold heavy-plunging foam,
Whirl'd by the wind, had roll'd me deep below,
    Then when I left my home.'

Her slow full words sank thro' the silence drear.
    As thunder-drops fall on a sleeping sea:
Sudden I heard a voice that cried, 'Come here,
    That I may look on thee.'

I turning saw, throned on a flowery rise,
    One sitting on a crimson scarf unroll'd;
A queen, with swarthy cheeks and bold black eyes,
    Brow-bound with burning gold.

She, flashing forth a haughty smile, began:
> 'I govern'd men by change, and so I sway'd
All moods. 'Tis long since I have seen a man.
> Once, like the moon, I made

'The ever-shifting currents of the blood
> According to my humour ebb and flow.
I have no men to govern in this wood:
> That makes my only woe.

'Nay – yet it chafes me that I could not bend
> One will; nor tame and tutor with mine eye
That dull cold-blooded Cæsar. Prythee, friend,
> Where is Mark Antony?

'The man, my lover, with whom I rode sublime
> On Fortune's neck: we sat as God by God:
The Nilus would have risen before his time
> And flooded at our nod.

'We drank the Libyan Sun to sleep, and lit
> Lamps which outburn'd Canopus. O my life
In Egypt! O the dalliance and the wit,
> The flattery and the strife,

'And the wild kiss, when fresh from war's alarms,
> My Hercules, my Roman Antony,
My mailed Bacchus leapt into my arms.
> Contented there to die!

'And there he died: and when I heard my name
> Sigh'd forth with life I would not brook fear

Of the other: with a worm I balk'd his fame.
    What else was left? look here!'

(With that she tore her robe apart, and half
    The polish'd argent of her breast to sight
Laid bare. Thereto she pointed with a laugh,
    Showing the aspick's bite.)

'I died a Queen. The Roman soldier found
    Me lying dead, my crown about my brows,
A name for ever! – lying robed and crown'd.
    Worthy a Roman spouse.'

Her warbling voice, a lyre of widest range
    Struck by all passion, did fall down and glance
From tone to tone, and glided thro' all change
    Of liveliest utterance.

When she made pause I knew not for delight;
    Because with sudden motion from the ground
She raised her piercing orbs, and fill'd with light
    The interval of sound.

Still with their fires Love tipt his keenest darts;
    As once they drew into two burning rings
All beams of Love, melting the mighty hearts
    Of captains and of kings.

Slowly my sense undazzled. Then I heard
    A noise of some one coming thro' the lawn,
And singing clearer than the crested bird,
    That claps his wings at dawn.

'The torrent brooks of hallow'd Israel
>From craggy hollows pouring, late and soon,
Sound all night long, in falling thro' the dell,
> Far-heard beneath the moon.

'The balmy moon of blessed Israel
> Floods all the deep-blue gloom with beams divine:
All night the splinter'd crags that wall the dell
> With spires of silver shine.'

As one that museth where broad sunshine laves
> The lawn by some cathedral, thro' the door
Hearing the holy organ rolling waves
> Of sound on roof and floor

Within, and anthem sung, is charm'd and tied
> To where he stands, – so stood I, when that flow
Of music left the lips of her that died
> To save her father's vow;

The daughter of the warrior Gileadite,
> A maiden pure; as when she went along
From Mizpeh's tower'd gate with welcome light,
> With timbrel and with song.

My words leapt forth: 'Heaven heads the count of crimes
> With that wild oath.' She render'd answer high:
'Not so, nor once alone; a thousand times
> I would be born and die.

'Single I grew, like some green plant, whose root
> Creeps to the garden water-pipes beneath,

Feeding the flower; but ere my flower to fruit
    Changed, I was ripe for death.

'My God, my land, my father – these did move
    Me from my bliss of life, that Nature gave,
Lower'd softly with a threefold cord of love
    Down to a silent grave.

'And I went mourning, "No fair Hebrew boy
    Shall smile away my maiden blame among
The Hebrew mothers" – emptied of all joy,
    Leaving the dance and song,

'Leaving the olive-gardens far below,
    Leaving the promise of my bridal bower,
The valleys of grape-loaded vines that glow
    Beneath the battled tower.

'The light white cloud swam over us. Anon
    We heard the lion roaring from his den;
We saw the large white stars rise one by one,
    Or, from the darken'd glen,

'Saw God divide the night with flying flame,
    And thunder on the everlasting hills.
I heard Him, for He spake, and grief became
    A solemn scorn of ills.

'When the next moon was roll'd into the sky,
    Strength came to me that equall'd my desire.
How beautiful a thing it was to die
    For God and for my sire!

'It comforts me in this one thought to dwell,
  That I subdued me to my father's will;
Because the kiss he gave me, ere I fell,
  Sweetens the spirit still.

'Moreover it is written that my race
  Hew'd Ammon, hip and thigh, from Aroer
On Arnon unto Minneth.' Here her face
  Glow'd, as I look'd at her.

She lock'd her lips: she left me where I stood:
  'Glory to God,' she sang, and past afar,
Thridding the sombre boskage of the wood.
  Toward the morning-star.

Losing her carol I stood pensively,
  As one that from a casement leans his head.
When midnight bells cease ringing suddenly.
  And the old year is dead.

'Alas! alas!' a low voice, full of care,
  Murmur'd beside me: 'Turn and look on me
I am that Rosamond, whom men call fair.
  If what I was I be.

'Would I had been some maiden coarse and poor!
  O me, that I should ever see the light!
Those dragon eyes of anger'd Eleanor
  Do hunt me, day and night.'

She ceased in tears, fallen from hope and trust:
  To whom the Egyptian: 'O, you tamely died!

You should have clung to Fulvia's waist, and thrust
> The dagger thro' her side.'

With that sharp sound the white dawn's creeping beams,
> Stol'n to my brain, dissolved the mystery

Of folded sleep. The captain of my dreams
> Ruled in the eastern sky.

Morn broaden'd on the borders of the dark.
> Ere I saw her, who clasp'd in her last trance

Her murder'd father's head, or Joan of Arc,
> A light of ancient France;

Or her, who knew that Love can vanquish Death,
> Who kneeling, with one arm about her king,

Drew forth the poison with her balmy breath,
> Sweet as new buds in Spring.

No memory labours longer from the deep
> Gold-mines of thought to lift the hidden ore

That glimpses, moving up, than I from sleep
> To gather and tell o'er

Each little sound and sight. With what dull pain
> Compass'd, how eagerly I sought to strike

Into that wondrous track of dreams again!
> But no two dreams are like.

As when a soul laments, which hath been blest,
> Desiring what is mingled with past years.

In yearnings that can never be exprest
> By sighs or groans or tears;

Because all words, tho' cull'd with choicest art,
    Failing to give the bitter of the sweet.
Wither beneath the palate, and the heart
    Faints, faded by its heat.

The Palace of Art

I built my soul a lordly pleasure-house,
    Wherein at ease for aye to dwell.
I said, 'O Soul, make merry and carouse,
    Dear soul, for all is well.'

A huge crag-platform, smooth as burnish'd brass,
    I chose. The ranged ramparts bright
From level meadow-bases of deep grass
    Suddenly scaled the light.

Thereon I built it firm. Of ledge or shelf
    The rock rose clear, or winding stair.
My soul would live alone unto herself
    In her high palace there.

And 'while the world runs round and round,' I said,
    'Reign thou apart, a quiet king,
Still as, while Saturn whirls, his steadfast shade
    Sleeps on his luminous ring.'

To which my soul made answer readily:
    'Trust me, in bliss I shall abide
In this great mansion, that is built for me,
    So royal-rich and wide.'

✥ ✥ ✥ ✥ ✥

Four courts I made, East, West and South and North,
    In each a squared lawn, wherefrom

The golden gorge of dragons spouted forth
    A flood of fountain-foam.

And round the cool green courts there ran a row
    Of cloisters, branch'd like mighty woods,
Echoing all night to that sonorous flow
    Of spouted fountain-floods.

And round the roofs a gilded gallery
    That lent broad verge to distant lands,
Far as the wild swan wings, to where the sky
    Dipt down to sea and sands.

From those four jets four currents in one swell
    Across the mountain stream'd below
In misty folds, that floating as they fell
    Lit up a torrent-bow.

And high on every peak a statue seem'd
    To hang on tiptoe, tossing up
A cloud of incense of all odour steam'd
    From out a golden cup.

So that she thought, 'And who shall gaze upon
    My palace with unblinded eyes,
While this great bow will waver in the sun,
    And that sweet incense rise?'

For that sweet incense rose and never fail'd,
    And, while day sank or mounted higher,
The light aerial gallery, golden-rail'd,
    Burnt like a fringe of fire.

Likewise the deep-set windows, stain'd and traced,
    Would seem slow-flaming crimson fires
From shadow'd grots of arches interlaced,
    And tipt with frost-like spires.

✥ ✥ ✥ ✥ ✥

Full of long-sounding corridors it was,
    That over-vaulted grateful gloom,
Thro' which the livelong day my soul did pass,
    Well-pleased, from room to room.

Full of great rooms and small the palace stood,
    All various, each a perfect whole
From living Nature, fit for every mood
    And change of my still soul.

For some were hung with arras green and blue,
    Showing a gaudy summer-morn,
Where with puff'd cheek the belted hunter blew
    His wreathed bugle-horn.

One seemed all dark and red – a tract of sand,
    And some one pacing there alone,
Who paced for ever in a glimmering land,
    Lit with a low large moon.

One showed an iron coast and angry waves.
    You seemed to hear them climb and fall
And roar rock-thwarted under bellowing caves,
    Beneath the windy wall.

And one, a full-fed river winding slow
    By herds upon an endless plain,
The ragged rims of thunder brooding low,
    With shadow-streaks of rain.

And one, the reapers at their sultry toil,
    In front they bound the sheaves. Behind
Were realms of upland, prodigal in oil,
    And hoary to the wind.

And one, a foreground black with stones and slags,
    Beyond, a line of heights, and higher
All barr'd with long white cloud the scornful crags,
    And highest, snow and fire.

And one, an English home – gray twilight pour'd
    On dewy pastures, dewy trees,
Softer than sleep – all things in order stored,
    A haunt of ancient Peace.

Nor these alone, but every landscape fair,
    As fit for every mood of mind,
Or gay, or grave, or sweet, or stern, was there,
    Not less than truth design'd.

✥ ✥ ✥ ✥ ✥

Or the maid-mother by a crucifix,
    In tracts of pasture sunny-warm.
Beneath branch-work of costly sardonyx
    Sat smiling, babe in arm.

Or in a clear-wall'd city on the sea,
    Near gilded organ-pipes, her hair
Wound with white roses, slept Saint Cecily;
    An angel look'd at her.

Or thronging all one porch of Paradise
    A group of Houris bow'd to see
The dying Islamite, with hands and eyes
    That said, We wait for thee.

Or mythic Uther's deeply-wounded son
    In some fair space of sloping greens
Lay, dozing in the vale of Avalon,
    And watch'd by weeping queens.

Or hollowing one hand against his ear,
    To list a foot-fall, ere he saw
The wood-nymph, stay'd the Ausonian king to hear
    Of wisdom and of law.

Or over hills with peaky tops engrail'd,
    And many a tract of palm and rice,
The throne of Indian Cama slowly sail'd
    A summer fann'd with spice.

Or sweet Europa's mantle blew unclasp'd,
    From off her shoulder backward borne:
From one hand droop'd a crocus: one hand grasp'd
    The mild bull's golden horn.

Or else flushed Ganymede, his rosy thigh
    Half-buried in the Eagle's down,

Sole as a flying star shot thro' the sky
    Above the pillar'd town.

Nor these alone: but every legend fair
    Which the supreme Caucasian mind
Carved out of Nature for itself, was there,
    Not less than life, design'd.

✥ ✥ ✥ ✥ ✥

Then in the towers I placed great bells that swung,
    Moved of themselves, with silver sound;
And with choice paintings of wise men I hung
    The royal dais round.

For there was Milton like a seraph strong,
    Beside him Shakespeare bland and mild;
And there the world-worn Dante grasp'd his song,
    And somewhat grimly smiled.

And there the Ionian father of the rest;
    A million wrinkles carved his skin;
A hundred winters snow'd upon his breast,
    From cheek and throat and chin.

Above, the fair hall-ceiling stately-set
    Many an arch high up did lift,
And angels rising and descending met
    With interchange of gift.

Below was all mosaic choicely plann'd
    With cycles of the human tale

Of this wide world, the times of every land
>	So wrought they will not fail.

The people here, a beast of burden slow,
>	Toil'd onward, prick'd with goads and stings;
Here play'd, a tiger, rolling to and fro
>	The heads and crowns of kings;

Here rose, an athlete, strong to break or bind
>	All force in bonds that might endure,
And here once more like some sick man declined,
>	And trusted any cure.

But over these she trod: and those great bells
>	Began to chime. She took her throne:
She sat betwixt the shining Oriels,
>	To sing her songs alone.

And thro' the topmost Oriels' coloured flame
>	Two godlike faces gazed below;
Plato the wise, and large-brow'd Verulam,
>	The first of those who know.

And all those names that in their motion were
>	Full-welling fountain-heads of change,
Betwixt the slender shafts were blazon'd fair
>	In diverse raiment strange:

Thro' which the lights, rose, amber, emerald, blue,
>	Flush'd in her temples and her eyes,
And from her lips, as morn from Memnon, drew
>	Rivers of melodies.

No nightingale delighteth to prolong
    Her low preamble all alone,
More than my soul to hear her echo'd song
    Throb thro' the ribbed stone;

Singing and murmuring in her feastful mirth,
    Joying to feel herself alive,
Lord over Nature, Lord of the visible earth,
    Lord of the senses five;
Communing with herself: 'All these are mine,
    And let the world have peace or wars,
'Tis one to me.' She – when young night divine
    Crown'd dying day with stars,

Making sweet close of his delicious toils –
    Lit light in wreaths and anadems,
And pure quintessences of precious oils
    In hollow'd moons of gems,

To mimic heaven; and clapt her hands and cried,
    'I marvel if my still delight
In this great house so royal-rich, and wide,
    Be flatter'd to the height.

'O all things fair to sate my various eyes!
    O shapes and hues that please me well!
O silent faces of the Great and Wise,
    My Gods, with whom I dwell!

'O God-like isolation which art mine,
    I can but count thee perfect gain,

What time I watch the darkening droves of swine
    That range on yonder plain.

'In filthy sloughs they roll a prurient skin,
    They graze and wallow, breed and sleep;
And oft some brainless devil enters in,
    And drives them to the deep.'

Then of the moral instinct would she prate
    And of the rising from the dead,
As hers by right of full-accomplish'd Fate;
    And at the last she said:

'I take possession of man's mind and deed.
    I care not what the sects may brawl.
I sit as God holding no form of creed,
    But contemplating all.'

✣ ✣ ✣ ✣ ✣

Full oft the riddle of the painful earth
    Flash'd thro' her as she sat alone,
Yet not the less held she her solemn mirth,
    And intellectual throne

And so she throve and prosper'd: so three years
    She prosper'd; on the fourth she fell,
Like Herod, when the shout was in his ears,
    Struck through with pangs of hell.

Lest she should fail and perish utterly,
    God, before whom ever lie bare

The abysmal deeps of Personality,
    Plagued her with sore despair.

When she would think, where'er she turn'd her sight
    The airy hand confusion wrought,
Wrote, 'Mene, mene,' and divided quite
    The kingdom of her thought.

Deep dread and loathing of her solitude
    Fell on her, from which mood was born
Scorn of herself; again, from out that mood
    Laughter at her self-scorn.

'What! is not this my place of strength,' she said,
    'My spacious mansion built for me,
Whereof the strong foundation-stones were laid
    Since my first memory?'

But in dark corners of her palace stood
    Uncertain shapes; and unawares
On white-eyed phantasms weeping tears of blood,
    And horrible nightmares,

And hollow shades enclosing hearts of flame,
    And, with dim fretted foreheads all,
On corpses three-months-old at noon she came,
    That stood against the wall.

A spot of dull stagnation, without light
    Or power of movement, seem'd my soul,
'Mid onward-sloping motions infinite
    Making for one sure goal.

A still salt pool, lock'd in with bars of sand,
    Left on the shore; that hears all night
The plunging seas draw backward from the land
    Their moon-led waters white.

A star that with the choral starry dance
    Join'd not, but stood, and standing saw
The hollow orb of moving Circumstance
    Roll'd round by one fix'd law.

Back on herself her serpent pride had curl'd.
    'No voice,' she shriek'd in that lone hall,
'No voice breaks thro' the stillness of this world:
    One deep, deep silence all!'

She, mouldering with the dull earth's mouldering sod,
    Inwrapt tenfold in slothful shame,
Lay there exiled from eternal God,
    Lost to her place and name;

And death and life she hated equally,
    And nothing saw, for her despair,
But dreadful time, dreadful eternity,
    No comfort anywhere;

Remaining utterly confused with fears,
    And ever worse with growing time,
And ever unrelieved by dismal tears,
    And all alone in crime:

Shut up as in a crumbling tomb, girt round
    With blackness as a solid wall,

Far off she seem'd to hear the dully sound
    Of human footsteps fall.

As in strange lands a traveller walking slow,
    In doubt and great perplexity,
A little before moon-rise hears the low
    Moan of an unknown sea;

And knows not if it be thunder, or a sound
    Of rocks thrown down, or one deep cry
Of great wild beasts; then thinketh, 'I have found
    A new land, but I die.'

She howl'd aloud, 'I am on fire within.
    There comes no murmur of reply.
What is it that will take away my sin,
    And save me lest I die?'

So when four years were wholly finished,
    She threw her royal robes away.
'Make me a cottage in the vale,' she said,
    'Where I may mourn and pray.

'Yet pull not down my palace towers, that are
    So lightly, beautifully built.
Perchance I may return with others there
    When I have purged my guilt.'

Mariana in the South

With one black shadow at its feet,
    The house thro' all the level shines,
Close-latticed to the brooding heat,
    And silent in its dusty vines:
A faint-blue ridge upon the right,
    An empty river-bed before,
    And shallows on a distant shore,
In glaring sand and inlets bright.
    But 'Ave Mary,' made she moan,
        And 'Ave Mary,' night and morn,
    And 'Ah,' she sang, 'to be all alone,
        To live forgotten, and love forlorn.'

She, as her carol sadder grew,
    From brow and bosom slowly down
Thro' rosy taper fingers drew
    Her streaming curls of deepest brown
To left and right, and made appear,
    Still-lighted in a secret shrine,
    Her melancholy eyes divine,
The home of woe without a tear.
    And 'Ave Mary,' was her moan,
        'Madonna, sad is night and morn,'
    And 'Ah,' she sang, 'to be all alone,
        To live forgotten, and love forlorn.'

Till all the crimson changed, and past
    Into deep orange o'er the sea,
Low on her knees herself she cast,
    Before Our Lady murmur'd she:

Complaining, 'Mother, give me grace
    To help me of my weary load.'
    And on the liquid mirror glow'd
The clear perfection of her face.
    'Is this the form,' she made her moan,
        'That won his praises night and morn?'
    And 'Ah,' she said, 'but I wake alone,
        I sleep forgotten, I wake forlorn.'

Nor bird would sing, nor lamb would bleat,
    Nor any cloud would cross the vault,
But day increased from heat to heat,
    On stony drought and steaming salt;
Till now at noon she slept again,
    And seem'd knee-deep in mountain grass,
    And heard her native breezes pass,
And runlets babbling down the glen.
    She breathed in sleep a lower moan,
        And murmuring, as at night and morn
    She thought, 'My spirit is here alone,
        Walks forgotten, and is forlorn.'

Dreaming, she knew it was a dream:
    She felt he was and was not there.
She woke: the babble of the stream
    Fell, and, without, the steady glare
Shrank one sick willow sere and small.
    The river-bed was dusty-white;
    And all the furnace of the light
Struck up against the blinding wall.
    She whisper'd, with a stifled moan
        More inward than at night or morn,

'Sweet Mother, let me not here alone
    Live forgotten and die forlorn.'

And, rising, from her bosom drew
    Old letters, breathing of her worth,
For 'Love', they said, 'must needs be true,
    To what is loveliest upon earth.'
An image seem'd to pass the door,
    To look at her with slight, and say,
    'But now thy beauty flows away,
So be alone for evermore.'
    'O cruel heart,' she changed her tone,
        'And cruel love, whose end is scorn,
    Is this the end to be left alone,
        To live forgotten, and die forlorn?'

But sometimes in the falling day
    An image seem'd to pass the door,
To look into her eyes and say,
    'But thou shalt be alone no more.'
And flaming downward over all
    From heat to heat the day decreased,
    And slowly rounded to the east
The one black shadow from the wall.
    'The day to night,' she made her moan,
        'The day to night, the night to morn,
    And day and night I am left alone
        To live forgotten, and love forlorn.'

At eve a dry cicala sung,
    There came a sound as of the sea;
Backward the lattice-blind she flung,

  And lean'd upon the balcony.
There all in spaces rosy-bright
  Large Hesper glitter'd on her tears,
  And deepening thro' the silent spheres
Heaven over Heaven rose the night.
  And weeping then she made her moan,
   'The night comes on that knows not morn,
  When I shall cease to be all alone,
   To live forgotten, and love forlorn.'

The Lotos Eaters

'Courage!' he said, and pointed toward the land,
'This mounting wave will roll us shoreward soon.'
In the afternoon they came unto a land
In which it seemed always afternoon.
All round the coast the languid air did swoon,
Breathing like one that hath a weary dream.
Full-faced above the valley stood the moon;
And like a downward smoke, the slender stream
Along the cliff to fall and pause and fall did
   seem.

A land of streams! some, like a downward smoke,
Slow-dropping veils of thinnest lawn, did go;
And some thro' wavering lights and shadows
   broke,
Rolling a slumbrous sheet of foam below.
They saw the gleaming river seaward flow
From the inner land: far off, three mountain-tops,
Three silent pinnacles of aged snow,
Stood sunset-flush'd: and, dew'd with showery
   drops,
Up-clomb the shadowy pine above the woven copse.

The charmed sunset linger'd low adown
In the red West: thro' mountain clefts the dale
Was seen far inland, and the yellow down
Border'd with palm, and many a winding vale
And meadow, set with slender galingale;
A land where all things always seem'd the same!
And round about the keel with faces pale,

Dark faces pale against that rosy flame,
The mild-eyed melancholy Lotos-eaters came.

Branches they bore of that enchanted stem,
Laden with flower and fruit, whereof they gave
To each, but whoso did receive of them,
And taste, to him the gushing of the wave
Far far away did seem to mourn and rave
On alien shores; and if his fellow spake,
His voice was thin, as voices from the grave;
And deep-asleep he seem'd, yet all awake,
And music in his ears his beating heart did make.

They sat them down upon the yellow sand,
Between the sun and moon upon the shore;
And sweet it was to dream of Fatherland,
Of child, and wife, and slave; but evermore
Most weary seem'd the sea, weary the oar,
Weary the wandering fields of barren foam.
Then some one said, 'We will return no more;'
And all at once they sang, 'Our island home
Is far beyond the wave; we will no longer roam.'

Choric Song

I

There is sweet music here that softer falls
Than petals from blown roses on the grass,
Or night-dews on still waters between walls
Of shadowy granite, in a gleaming pass;
Music that gentlier on the spirit lies,
Than tir'd eyelids upon tir'd eyes;
Music that brings sweet sleep down from the blissful
   skies.
Here are cool mosses deep,
And thro' the moss the ivies creep,
And in the stream the long-leaved flowers weep,
And from the craggy ledge the poppy hangs in
   sleep.

II

Why are we weigh'd upon with heaviness,
And utterly consumed with sharp distress,
While all things else have rest from weariness?
All things have rest: why should we toil alone,
We only toil, who are the first of things,
And make perpetual moan,
Still from one sorrow to another thrown:
Nor ever fold our wings,
And cease from wanderings,
Nor steep our brows in slumber's holy balm;
Nor harken what the inner spirit sings,
'There is no joy but calm!'
Why should we only toil, the roof and crown of
   things?

III

Lo! in the middle of the wood,
The folded leaf is woo'd from out the bud
With winds upon the branch, and there
Grows green and broad, and takes no care,
Sun-steep'd at noon, and in the moon
Nightly dew-fed; and turning yellow
Falls, and floats adown the air.
Lo! sweeten'd with the summer light,
The full-juiced apple, waxing over-mellow,
Drops in a silent autumn night.
All its allotted length of days
The flower ripens in its place,
Ripens and fades, and falls, and hath no toil,
Fast-rooted in the fruitful soil.

IV

Hateful is the dark-blue sky,
Vaulted o'er the dark-blue sea.
Death is the end of life; ah, why
Should life all labour be?
Let us alone. Time driveth onward fast,
And in a little while our lips are dumb.
Let us alone. What is it that will last?
All things are taken from us, and become
Portions and parcels of the dreadful past.
Let us alone. What pleasure can we have
To war with evil? Is there any peace
In ever climbing up the climbing wave?
All things have rest, and ripen toward the grave
In silence; ripen, fall and cease:
Give us long rest or death, dark death, or dreamful ease.

V

How sweet it were, hearing the downward stream,
With half-shut eyes ever to seem
Falling asleep in a half-dream!
To dream and dream, like yonder amber light,
Which will not leave the myrrh-bush on the height;
To hear each other's whisper'd speech;
Eating the Lotos day by day,
To watch the crisping ripples on the beach,
And tender curving lines of creamy spray;
To lend our hearts and spirits wholly
To the influence of mild-minded melancholy;
To muse and brood and live again in memory,
With those old faces of our infancy
Heap'd over with a mound of grass,
Two handfuls of white dust, shut in an urn of brass!

VI

Dear is the memory of our wedded lives,
And dear the last embraces of our wives
And their warm tears: but all hath suffer'd change;
For surely now our household hearths are cold:
Our sons inherit us: our looks are strange:
And we should come like ghosts to trouble joy.
Or else the island princes over-bold
Have eat our substance, and the minstrel sings
Before them of the ten years' war in Troy,
And our great deeds, as half-forgotten things.
Is there confusion in the little isle?
Let what is broken so remain.
The Gods are hard to reconcile:
'Tis hard to settle order once again.

There *is* confusion worse than death,
Trouble on trouble, pain on pain,
Long labour unto aged breath,
Sore task to hearts worn out by many wars
And eyes grown dim with gazing on the pilot-stars.

VII

But, propt on beds of amaranth and moly,
How sweet (while warm airs lull us, blowing lowly)
With half-dropt eyelid still,
Beneath a heaven dark and holy,
To watch the long bright river drawing slowly
His waters from the purple hill –
To hear the dewy echoes calling
From cave to cave thro' the thick-twined vine –
To watch the emerald-colour'd water falling
Thro' many a wov'n acanthus-wreath divine!
Only to hear and see the far-off sparkling brine,
Only to hear were sweet, stretch'd out beneath the pine.

VIII

The Lotos blooms below the barren peak:
The Lotos blows by every winding creek:
All day the wind breathes low with mellower tone:
Thro' every hollow cave and alley lone
Round and round the spicy downs the yellow Lotos-dust
  is blown.
We have had enough of action, and of motion we,
Roll'd to starboard, roll'd to larboard, when the surge was
  seething free,
Where the wallowing monster spouted his foam-fountains
  in the sea.

Let us swear an oath, and keep it with an equal mind,
In the hollow Lotos-land to live and lie reclined
On the hills like Gods together, careless of mankind.
For they lie beside their nectar, and the bolts are hurl'd
Far below them in the valleys, and the clouds are lightly curl'd
Round their golden houses, girdled with the gleaming world:
Where they smile in secret, looking over wasted lands,
Blight and famine, plague and earthquake, roaring deeps and fiery sands,
Clanging fights, and flaming towns, and sinking ships, and praying hands.
But they smile, they find a music centred in a doleful song
Steaming up, a lamentation and an ancient tale of wrong,
Like a tale of little meaning tho' the words are strong;
Chanted from an ill-used race of men that cleave the soil,
Sow the seed, and reap the harvest with enduring toil,
Storing yearly little dues of wheat, and wine and oil;
Till they perish and they suffer – some, 'tis whisper'd – down in hell
Suffer endless anguish, others in Elysian valleys dwell,
Resting weary limbs at last on beds of asphodel.
Surely, surely, slumber is more sweet than toil, the shore
Than labour in the deep mid-ocean, wind and wave and oar;
O, rest ye, brother mariners, we will not wander more.

St Simeon Stylites

Altho' I be the basest of mankind,
From scalp to sole one slough and crust of sin,
Unfit for earth, unfit for heaven, scarce meet
For troops of devils, mad with blasphemy,
I will not cease to grasp the hope I hold
Of saintdom, and to clamour, mourn and sob,
Battering the gates of heaven with storms of prayer,
Have mercy, Lord, and take away my sin.

    Let this avail, just, dreadful, mighty God,
This not be all in vain, that thrice ten years,
Thrice multiplied by superhuman pangs,
In hungers and in thirsts, fevers and cold,
In coughs, aches, stitches, ulcerous throes and cramps,
A sign betwixt the meadow and the cloud,
Patient on this tall pillar I have borne
Rain, wind, frost, heat, hail, damp, and sleet, and snow;
And I had hoped that ere this period closed
Thou wouldst have caught me up into thy rest,
Denying not these weather-beaten limbs
The meed of saints, the white robe and the palm.

    O take the meaning, Lord: I do not breathe,
Not whisper, any murmur of complaint.
Pain heaped ten-hundred-fold to this, were still
Less burthen, by ten-hundred-fold, to bear,
Than were those lead-like tons of sin that crushed
My spirit flat before thee.
                      O Lord, Lord,
Thou knowest I bore this better at the first,

For I was strong and hale of body then;
And tho' my teeth, which now are dropped away,
Would chatter with the cold, and all my beard
Was tagg'd with icy fringes in the moon,
I drown'd the whoopings of the owl with sound
Of pious hymns and psalms, and sometimes saw
An angel stand and watch me, as I sang.
Now am I feeble grown; my end draws nigh;
I hope my end draws nigh: half deaf I am,
So that I scarce can hear the people hum
About the column's base, and almost blind,
And scarce can recognise the fields I know;
And both my thighs are rotted with the dew;
Yet cease I not to clamour and to cry,
While my stiff spine can hold my weary head,
Till all my limbs drop piecemeal from the stone,
Have mercy, mercy: take away my sin.

    O Jesus, if thou wilt not save my soul,
Who may be saved? who is it may be saved?
Who may be made a saint, if I fail here?
Show me the man hath suffer'd more than I.
For did not all thy martyrs die one death?
For either they were stoned, or crucified,
Or burn'd in fire, or boil'd in oil, or sawn
In twain beneath the ribs; but I die here
Today, and whole years long, a life of death.
Bear witness, if I could have found a way
(And heedfully I sifted all my thought)
More slowly-painful to subdue this home
Of sin, my flesh, which I despise and hate,
I had not stinted practice, O my God.

    For not alone this pillar-punishment,
Not this alone I bore: but while I lived
In the white convent down the valley there,
For many weeks about my loins I wore
The rope that haled the buckets from the well,
Twisted as tight as I could knot the noose;
And spake not of it to a single soul,
Until the ulcer, eating thro' my skin,
Betray'd my secret penance, so that all
My brethren marvelled greatly. More than this
I bore, whereof, O God, thou knowest all.

    Three winters, that my soul might grow to thee,
I lived up there on yonder mountain side.
My right leg chained into the crag, I lay
Pent in a roofless close of ragged stones;
Inswathed sometimes in wandering mist, and twice
Blacked with thy branding thunder, and sometimes
Sucking the damps for drink, and eating not,
Except the spare chance-gift of those that came
To touch my body and be healed, and live:
And they say then that I worked miracles,
Whereof my fame is loud amongst mankind,
Cured lameness, palsies, cancers. Thou, O God,
Knowest alone whether this was or no.
Have mercy, mercy! cover all my sin.

    Then, that I might be more alone with thee,
Three years I lived upon a pillar, high
Six cubits, and three years on one of twelve;
And twice three years I crouched on one that rose

Twenty by measure; last of all, I grew
Twice ten long weary weary years to this,
That numbers forty cubits from the soil.

    I think that I have borne as much as this –
Or else I dream – and for so long a time,
If I may measure time by yon slow light,
And this high dial, which my sorrow crowns –
So much – even so.
                   And yet I know not well,
For that the evil ones come here, and say,
'Fall down, O Simeon: thou hast suffer'd long
For ages and for ages!' then they prate
Of penances I cannot have gone thro',
Perplexing me with lies; and oft I fall,
Maybe for months, in such blind lethargies
That Heaven, and Earth, and Time are choked.
                                           But yet
Bethink thee, Lord, while thou and all the saints
Enjoy themselves in heaven, and men on earth
House in the shade of comfortable roofs,
Sit with their wives by fires, eat wholesome food,
And wear warm clothes, and even beasts have stalls,
I, 'tween the spring and downfall of the light,
Bow down one thousand and two hundred times,
To Christ, the Virgin Mother, and the saints;
Or in the night, after a little sleep,
I wake: the chill stars sparkle; I am wet
With drenching dews, or stiff with crackling frost.
I wear an undress'd goatskin on my back;
A grazing iron collar grinds my neck;

And in my weak lean arms I lift the cross,
And strive and wrestle with thee till I die:
O mercy, mercy! wash away my sin.

    O Lord, thou knowest what a man I am;
A sinful man, conceived and born in sin:
'Tis their own doing; this is none of mine;
Lay it not to me. Am I to blame for this,
That here come those that worship me? Ha! ha!
They think that I am somewhat. What am I?
The silly people take me for a saint,
And bring me offerings of fruit and flowers:
And I, in truth (thou wilt bear witness here)
Have all in all endured as much, and more,
Than many just and holy men, whose names
Are register'd and calendar'd for saints.

    Good people, you do ill to kneel to me.
What is it I can have done to merit this?
I am a sinner viler than you all.
It may be I have wrought some miracles,
And cured some halt and maim'd; but what of that?
It may be, no one, even among the saints,
May match his pains with mine; but what of that?
Yet do not rise; for you may look on me,
And in your looking you may kneel to God.
Speak! is there any of you halt or maim'd?
I think you know I have some power with Heaven
From my long penance: let him speak his wish.

    Yes, I can heal him. Power goes forth from me.
They say that they are heal'd. Ah, hark! they shout

'St Simeon Stylites.' Why, if so,
God reaps a harvest in me! O my soul,
God reaps a harvest in thee. If this be,
Can I work miracles and not be saved?
This is not told of any. They were saints.
It cannot be but that I shall be saved;
Yea, crowned a saint. They shout, 'Behold a saint!'
And lower voices saint me from above.
Courage, St Simeon! This dull chrysalis
Cracks into shining wings, and hope ere death
Spreads more and more and more, that God hath now
Sponged and made blank of crimeful record all
My mortal archives.
     O my sons, my sons,
I, Simeon of the pillar, by surname
Stylites, among men; I, Simeon,
The watcher on the column till the end;
I, Simeon, whose brain the sunshine bakes;
I, whose bald brows in silent hours become
Unnaturally hoar with rime, do now
From my high nest of penance here proclaim
That Pontius and Iscariot by my side
Show'd like fair seraphs. On the coals I lay,
A vessel full of sin: all hell beneath
Made me boil over. Devils pluck'd my sleeve,
Abaddon and Asmodeus caught at me.
I smote them with the cross; they swarm'd again.
In bed like monstrous apes they crushed my chest:
They flapp'd my light out as I read: I saw
Their faces grow between me and my book;
With colt-like whinny and with hoggish whine
They burst my prayer. Yet this way was left,

And by this way I 'scaped them. Mortify
Your flesh, like me, with scourges and with thorns;
Smite, shrink not, spare not. If it may be, fast
Whole Lents, and pray. I hardly, with slow steps,
With slow, faint steps, and much exceeding pain,
Have scrambled past those pits of fire, that still
Sing in mine ears. But yield not me the praise:
God only thro' his bounty hath thought fit,
Among the powers and princes of this world,
To make me an example to mankind,
Which few can reach to. Yet I do not say
But that a time may come — yea, even now,
Now, now, his footsteps smite the threshold stairs
Of life — I say, that time is at the doors
When you may worship me without reproach;
For I will leave my relics in your land,
And you may carve a shrine about my dust,
And burn a fragrant lamp before my bones,
When I am gather'd to the glorious saints.

    While I spake then, a sting of shrewdest pain
Ran shrivelling thro' me, and a cloudlike change,
In passing, with a grosser film made thick
These heavy, horny eyes. The end! the end!
Surely the end! What's here? a shape, a shade,
A flash of light. Is that the angel there
That holds a crown? Come, blessed brother, come.
I know thy glittering face. I waited long;
My brows are ready. What! deny it now?
Nay, draw, draw, draw nigh. So I clutch it. Christ!
'Tis gone: 'tis here again; the crown! the crown!
So now 'tis fitted on and grows to me,

And from it melt the dews of Paradise,
Sweet! sweet! spikenard, and balm, and frankincense.
Ah! let me not be fooled, sweet saints: I trust
That I am whole, and clean, and meet for Heaven.

    Speak, if there be a priest, a man of God,
Among you there, and let him presently
Approach, and lean a ladder on the shaft,
And climbing up into my airy home,
Deliver me the blessed sacrament;
For by the warning of the Holy Ghost,
I prophesy that I shall die to-night,
A quarter before twelve.
                     But thou, O Lord,
Aid all this foolish people; let them take
Example, pattern: lead them to thy light.

Ulysses

It little profits that an idle king,
By this still hearth, among these barren crags,
Match'd with an aged wife, I mete and dole
Unequal laws unto a savage race,
That hoard, and sleep, and feed, and know not me.

I cannot rest from travel: I will drink
Life to the lees: all times I have enjoy'd
Greatly, have suffer'd greatly, both with those
That loved me, and alone, on shore, and when
Thro' scudding drifts the rainy Hyades
Vext the dim sea: I am become a name;
For always roaming with a hungry heart
Much have I seen and known; cities of men
And manners, climates, councils, governments,
Myself not least, but honour'd of them all;
And drunk delight of battle with my peers,
Far on the ringing plains of windy Troy.
I am a part of all that I have met;
Yet all experience is an arch wherethro'
Gleams that untravell'd world whose margin fades
For ever and forever when I move.
How dull it is to pause, to make an end,
To rust unburnish'd, not to shine in use!
As tho' to breathe were life! Life piled on life
Were all too little, and of one to me
Little remains: but every hour is saved
From that eternal silence, something more,
A bringer of new things; and vile it were
For some three suns to store and hoard myself,

And this gray spirit yearning in desire
To follow knowledge like a sinking star,
Beyond the utmost bound of human thought.

    This is my son, mine own Telemachus,
To whom I leave the sceptre and the isle, –
Well-loved of me, discerning to fulfil
This labour, by slow prudence to make mild
A rugged people, and thro' soft degrees
Subdue them to the useful and the good.
Most blameless is he, centred in the sphere
Of common duties, decent not to fail
In offices of tenderness, and pay
Meet adoration to my household gods,
When I am gone. He works his work, I mine.

    There lies the port; the vessel puffs her sail:
There gloom the dark, broad seas. My mariners,
Souls that have toil'd, and wrought, and thought with
    me –
That ever with a frolic welcome took
The thunder and the sunshine, and opposed
Free hearts, free foreheads – you and I are old;
Old age hath yet his honour and his toil;
Death closes all: but something ere the end,
Some work of noble note, may yet be done,
Not unbecoming men that strove with Gods.
The lights begin to twinkle from the rocks:
The long day wanes: the slow moon climbs: the deep
Moans round with many voices. Come, my friends,
'Tis not too late to seek a newer world.
Push off, and sitting well in order smite

The sounding furrows; for my purpose holds
To sail beyond the sunset, and the baths
Of all the western stars, until I die.
It may be that the gulfs will wash us down:
It may be we shall touch the Happy Isles,
And see the great Achilles, whom we knew.
Tho' much is taken, much abides; and tho'
We are not now that strength which in old days
Moved earth and heaven, that which we are, we are;
One equal temper of heroic hearts,
Made weak by time and fate, but strong in will
To strive, to seek, to find, and not to yield.

The Two Voices

A still small voice spake unto me,
'Thou art so full of misery,
Were it not better not to be?'

Then to the still small voice I said;
'Let me not cast in endless shade
What is so wonderfully made.'

To which the voice did urge reply,
'To-day I saw the dragon-fly
Come from the wells where he did lie.

'An inner impulse rent the veil
Of his old husk: from head to tail
Came out clear plates of sapphire mail.

'He dried his wings: like gauze they grew:
Thro' crofts and pastures wet with dew
A living flash of light he flew.'

I said, 'When first the world began
Young Nature thro' five cycles ran,
And in the sixth she moulded man.

'She gave him mind, the lordliest
Proportion, and, above the rest,
Dominion in the head and breast.'

Thereto the silent voice replied;
'Self-blinded are you by your pride:
Look up thro' night: the world is wide.

'This truth within thy mind rehearse,
That in a boundless universe
Is boundless better, boundless worse.

'Think you this mould of hopes and fears
Could find no statelier than his peers
In yonder hundred million spheres?'

It spake, moreover, in my mind:
'Tho' thou wert scatter'd to the wind,
Yet is there plenty of the kind.'

Then did my response clearer fall:
'No compound of this earthly ball
Is like another, all in all.'

To which he answer'd scoffingly;
'Good soul! suppose I grant it thee,
Who'll weep for thy deficiency?

'Or will one beam be less intense,
When thy peculiar difference
Is cancell'd in the world of sense?'

I would have said, 'Thou canst not know,'
But my full heart, that work'd below,
Rain'd thro' my sight its overflow.

Again the voice spake unto me:
'Thou art so steep'd in misery,
Surely 'twere better not to be.

'Thine anguish will not let thee sleep,
Nor any train of reason keep:
Thou canst not think, but thou wilt weep.'

I said, 'The years with change advance:
If I make dark my countenance,
I shut my life from happier chance.

'Some turn this sickness yet might take,
Ev'n yet.' But he: 'What drug can make
A wither'd palsy cease to shake?'

I wept, 'Tho' I should die, I know
That all about the thorn will blow
In tufts of rosy-tinted snow;

'And men, thro' novel spheres of thought
Still moving after truth long sought,
Will learn new things when I am not.'

'Yet,' said the secret voice, 'some time,
Sooner or later, will gray prime
Make thy grass hoar with early rime.

'Not less swift souls that yearn for light,
Rapt after heaven's starry flight,
Would sweep the tracts of day and night.

'Not less the bee would range her cells,
The furzy prickle fire the dells,
The foxglove cluster dappled bells.'

I said that 'all the years invent;
Each month is various to present
The world with some development.

'Were this not well, to bide mine hour,
Tho' watching from a ruin'd tower
How grows the day of human power?'

'The highest-mounted mind,' he said,
'Still sees the sacred morning spread
The silent summit overhead.

'Will thirty seasons render plain
Those lonely lights that still remain,
Just breaking over land and main?

'Or make that morn, from his cold crown
And crystal silence creeping down,
Flood with full daylight glebe and town?

'Forerun thy peers, thy time, and let
Thy feet, millenniums hence, be set
In midst of knowledge, dream'd not yet.

'Thou hast not gain'd a real height,
Nor art thou nearer to the light,
Because the scale is infinite.

"'Twere better not to breathe or speak,
Than cry for strength, remaining weak,
And seem to find, but still to seek.

'Moreover, but to seem to find
Asks what thou lackest, thought resign'd,
A healthy frame, a quiet mind.'

I said, 'When I am gone away,
'He dared not tarry,' men will say,
Doing dishonour to my clay.'

'This is more vile,' he made reply,
'To breathe and loathe, to live and sigh,
Than once from dread of pain to die.

'Sick art thou — a divided will
Still heaping on the fear of ill
The fear of men, a coward still.

'Do men love thee? Art thou so bound
To men, that how thy name may sound
Will vex thee lying underground?

'The memory of the wither'd leaf
In endless time is scarce more brief
Than of the garner'd Autumn-sheaf.

'Go, vexed Spirit, sleep in trust;
The right ear, that is fill'd with dust,
Hears little of the false or just.'

'Hard task, to pluck resolve,' I cried,
'From emptiness and the waste wide
Of that abyss, or scornful pride!

'Nay – rather yet that I could raise
One hope that warm'd me in the days
While still I yearn'd for human praise.

'When, wide in soul, and bold of tongue,
Among the tents I paused and sung,
The distant battle flash'd and rung.

'I sung the joyful Paean clear,
And, sitting, burnish'd without fear
The brand, the buckler, and the spear –

'Waiting to strive a happy strife,
To war with falsehood to the knife,
And not to lose the good of life –

'Some hidden principle to move,
To put together, part and prove,
And mete the bounds of hate and love –

'As far as might be, to carve out
Free space for every human doubt,
That the whole mind might orb about –

'To search thro' all I felt or saw,
The springs of life, the depths of awe,
And reach the law within the law:

'At least, not rotting like a weed,
But, having sown some generous seed,
Fruitful of further thought and deed,

'To pass, when Life her light withdraws,
Not void of righteous self-applause,
Nor in a merely selfish cause –

'In some good cause, not in mine own,
To perish, wept for, honour'd, known,
And like a warrior overthrown;

'Whose eyes are dim with glorious tears,
When, soil'd with noble dust, he hears
His country's war-song thrill his ears:

'Then dying of a mortal stroke,
What time the foeman's line is broke.
And all the war is roll'd in smoke.'

'Yea!' said the voice, 'thy dream was good,
While thou abodest in the bud.
It was the stirring of the blood.

'If Nature put not forth her power
About the opening of the flower,
Who is it that could live an hour?

'Then comes the check, the change, the fall.
Pain rises up, old pleasures pall.
There is one remedy for all.

'Yet hadst thou, thro' enduring pain,
Link'd month to month with such a chain
Of knitted purport, all were vain.

'Thou hadst not between death and birth
Dissolved the riddle of the earth.
So were thy labour little-worth.

'That men with knowledge merely play'd,
I told thee – hardly nigher made,
Tho' scaling slow from grade to grade;

'Much less this dreamer, deaf and blind,
Named man, may hope some truth to find,
That bears relation to the mind.

'For every worm beneath the moon
Draws different threads, and late and soon
Spins, toiling out his own cocoon.

'Cry, faint not: either Truth is born
Beyond the polar gleam forlorn,
Or in the gateways of the morn.

'Cry, faint not, climb: the summits slope
Beyond the furthest nights of hope,
Wrapt in dense cloud from base to cope.

'Sometimes a little corner shines,
As over rainy mist inclines
A gleaming crag with belts of pines.

'I will go forward, sayest thou,
I shall not fail to find her now.
Look up, the fold is on her brow.

'If straight thy track, or if oblique,
Thou know'st not. Shadows thou dost strike,
Embracing cloud, Ixion-like;

'And owning but a little more
Than beasts, abidest lame and poor,
Calling thyself a little lower

'Than angels. Cease to wail and brawl!
Why inch by inch to darkness crawl?
There is one remedy for all.'

'O dull, one-sided voice,' said I,
'Wilt thou make everything a lie,
To flatter me that I may die?

'I know that age to age succeeds,
Blowing a noise of tongues and deeds,
A dust of systems and of creeds.

'I cannot hide that some have striven,
Achieving calm, to whom was given
The joy that mixes man with Heaven:

'Who, rowing hard against the stream,
Saw distant gates of Eden gleam,
And did not dream it was a dream;

'But heard, by secret transport led,
Ev'n in the charnels of the dead,
The murmur of the fountain-head —

'Which did accomplish their desire,
Bore and forbore, and did not tire,
Like Stephen, an unquenched fire.

'He heeded not reviling tones,
Nor sold his heart to idle moans,
Tho' cursed and scorn'd, and bruised with stones:

'But looking upward, full of grace,
He pray'd, and from a happy place
God's glory smote him on the face.'

The sullen answer slid betwixt:
'Not that the grounds of hope were fix'd,
The elements were kindlier mix'd.'

I said, 'I toil beneath the curse,
But, knowing not the universe,
I fear to slide from bad to worse.

'And that, in seeking to undo
One riddle, and to find the true,
I knit a hundred others new:

'Or that this anguish fleeting hence,
Unmanacled from bonds of sense,
Be fix'd and froz'n to permanence:

'For I go, weak from suffering here;
Naked I go, and void of cheer:
What is it that I may not fear?'

'Consider well,' the voice replied,
'His face, that two hours since hath died;
Wilt thou find passion, pain or pride?

'Will he obey when one commands?
Or answer should one press his hands?
He answers not, nor understands.

'His palms are folded on his breast:
There is no other thing express'd
But long disquiet merged in rest.

'His lips are very mild and meek:
Tho' one should smite him on the cheek,
And on the mouth, he will not speak.

'His little daughter, whose sweet face
He kiss'd, taking his last embrace,
Becomes dishonour to her race –

'His sons grow up that bear his name,
Some grow to honour, some to shame, –
But he is chill to praise or blame.

'He will not hear the north-wind rave,
Nor, moaning, household shelter crave
From winter rains that beat his grave.

'High up the vapours fold and swim:
About him broods the twilight dim:
The place he knew forgetteth him.'

'If all be dark, vague voice,' I said,
'These things are wrapt in doubt and dread,
Nor canst thou show the dead are dead.

'The sap dries up: the plant declines.
A deeper tale my heart divines.
Know I not Death? the outward signs?

'I found him when my years were few;
A shadow on the graves I knew,
And darkness in the village yew.

'From grave to grave the shadow crept:
In her still place the morning wept:
Touch'd by his feet the daisy slept.

'The simple senses crown'd his head:
'Omega! thou art Lord,' they said,
'We find no motion in the dead.'

'Why, if man rot in dreamless ease,
Should that plain fact, as taught by these,
Not make him sure that he shall cease?

'Who forged that other influence,
That heat of inward evidence,
By which he doubts against the sense?

'He owns the fatal gift of eyes,
That read his spirit blindly wise,
Not simple as a thing that dies.

'Here sits he shaping wings to fly:
His heart forebodes a mystery:
He names the name Eternity.

'That type of Perfect in his mind
In Nature can he nowhere find.
He sows himself in every wind.

'He seems to hear a Heavenly Friend,
And thro' thick veils to apprehend
A labour working to an end.

'The end and the beginning vex
His reason: many things perplex,
With motions, checks, and counterchecks.

'He knows a baseness in his blood
At such strange war with something good,
He may not do the thing he would.

'Heaven opens inward, chasms yawn.
Vast images in glimmering dawn,
Half shown, are broken and withdrawn.

'Ah! sure within him and without,
Could his dark wisdom find it out,
There must be answer to his doubt.

'But thou canst answer not again.
With thine own weapon art thou slain,
Or thou wilt answer but in vain.

'The doubt would rest, I dare not solve.
In the same circle we revolve.
Assurance only breeds resolve.'

As when a billow, blown against,
Falls back, the voice with which I fenced
A little ceased, but recommenced.

'Where wert thou when thy father play'd
In his free field, and pastime made,
A merry boy in sun and shade?

'A merry boy they called him then.
He sat upon the knees of men
In days that never come again.

'Before the little ducts began
To feed thy bones with lime, and ran
Their course, till thou wert also man:

'Who took a wife, who rear'd his race,
Whose wrinkles gather'd on his face,
Whose troubles number with his days:

'A life of nothings, nothing-worth,
From that first nothing ere his birth
To that last nothing under earth!'

'These words,' I said, 'are like the rest,
No certain clearness, but at best
A vague suspicion of the breast:

'But if I grant, thou mightst defend
The thesis which thy words intend –
That to begin implies to end;

'Yet how should I for certain hold,
Because my memory is so cold,
That I first was in human mould?

'I cannot make this matter plain,
But I would shoot, howe'er in vain,
A random arrow from the brain.

'It may be that no life is found,
Which only to one engine bound
Falls off, but cycles always round.

'As old mythologies relate,
Some draught of Lethe might await
The slipping thro' from state to state.

'As here we find in trances, men
Forget the dream that happens then,
Until they fall in trance again.

'So might we, if our state were such
As one before, remember much,
For those two likes might meet and touch.

'But, if I lapsed from nobler place,
Some legend of a fallen race
Alone might hint of my disgrace;

'Some vague emotion of delight
In gazing up an Alpine height,
Some yearning toward the lamps of night;

'Or if thro' lower lives I came –
Tho' all experience past became
Consolidate in mind and frame –

'I might forget my weaker lot;
For is not our first year forgot?
The haunts of memory echo not.

'And men, whose reason long was blind,
From cells of madness unconfined,
Oft lose whole years of darker mind.

'Much more, if first I floated free,
As naked essence, must I be
Incompetent of memory:

'For memory dealing but with time,
And he with matter, could she climb
Beyond her own material prime?

'Moreover, something is or seems,
That touches me with mystic gleams,
Like glimpses of forgotten dreams –

'Of something felt, like something here;
Of something done, I know not where;
Such as no language may declare.'

The still voice laugh'd. 'I talk,' said he,
'Not with thy dreams. Suffice it thee
Thy pain is a reality.'

'But thou,' said I, 'hast miss'd thy mark,
Who sought'st to wreck my mortal ark,
By making all the horizon dark.

'Why not set forth, if I should do
This rashness, that which might ensue
With this old soul in organs new?

'Whatever crazy sorrow saith,
No life that breathes with human breath
Has ever truly long'd for death.

''Tis life, whereof our nerves are scant,
Oh life, not death, for which we pant;
More life, and fuller, that I want.'

I ceased, and sat as one forlorn.
Then said the voice, in quiet scorn,
'Behold it is the Sabbath morn.'

And I arose, and I released
The casement, and the light increased
With freshness in the dawning east.

Like soften'd airs that blowing steal,
When meres begin to uncongeal,
The sweet church bells began to peal.

On to God's house the people prest:
Passing the place where each must rest,
Each enter'd like a welcome guest.

One walk'd between his wife and child,
With measur'd footfall firm and mild,
And now and then he gravely smiled.

The prudent partner of his blood
Lean'd on him, faithful, gentle, good,
Wearing the rose of womanhood.

And in their double love secure,
The little maiden walk'd demure,
Pacing with downward eyelids pure.

These three made unity so sweet,
My frozen heart began to beat,
Remembering its ancient heat.

I blest them, and they wander'd on:
I spoke, but answer came there none:
The dull and bitter voice was gone.

A second voice was at mine ear,
A little whisper silver-clear,
A murmur, 'Be of better cheer.'

As from some blissful neighbourhood,
A notice faintly understood,
'I see the end, and know the good.'

A little hint to solace woe,
A hint, a whisper breathing low,
'I may not speak of what I know.'

Like an Æolian harp that wakes
No certain air, but overtakes
Far thought with music that it makes:

Such seem'd the whisper at my side:
'What is it thou knowest, sweet voice?' I cried.
'A hidden hope,' the voice replied:

So heavenly-toned, that in that hour
From out my sullen heart a power
Broke, like the rainbow from the shower,

To feel, altho' no tongue can prove,
That every cloud, that spreads above
And veileth love, itself is love.

And forth into the fields I went,
And Nature's living motion lent
The pulse of hope to discontent.

I wonder'd at the bounteous hours,
The slow result of winter showers:
You scarce could see the grass for flowers.

I wonder'd, while I paced along:
The woods were fill'd so full with song,
There seem'd no room for sense of wrong.

And all so variously wrought,
I marvell'd how the mind was brought
To anchor by one gloomy thought;

And wherefore rather I made choice
To commune with that barren voice,
Than him that said, 'Rejoice! Rejoice!'

Morte d'Arthur

So all day long the noise of battle roll'd
Among the mountains by the winter sea;
Until King Arthur's table, man by man,
Had fallen in Lyonnesse about their Lord,
King Arthur: then, because his wound was deep,
The bold Sir Bedivere uplifted him,
Sir Bedivere, the last of all his knights,
And bore him to a chapel nigh the field,
A broken chancel with a broken cross,
That stood on a dark strait of barren land.
On one side lay the ocean, and on one
Lay a great water, and the moon was full.

    Then spake King Arthur to Sir Bedivere:
'The sequel of to-day unsolders all
The goodliest fellowship of famous knights
Whereof this world holds record. Such a sleep
They sleep – the men I loved. I think that we
Shall never more, at any future time,
Delight our souls with talk of knightly deeds,
Walking about the gardens and the halls
Of Camelot, as in the days that were.
I perish by this people which I made, –
Tho' Merlin sware that I should come again
To rule once more – but let what will be, be,
I am so deeply smitten thro' the helm
That without help I cannot last till morn.
Thou therefore take my brand Excalibur,
Which was my pride: for thou rememberest how
In those old days, one summer noon, an arm

Rose up from out the bosom of the lake,
Clothed in white samite, mystic, wonderful,
Holding the sword – and how I row'd across
And took it, and have worn it, like a king:
And, wheresoever I am sung or told
In aftertime, this also shall be known:
But now delay not: take Excalibur,
And fling him far into the middle mere:
Watch what thou seëst, and lightly bring me word.'

To him replied the bold Sir Bedivere:
'It is not meet, Sir King, to leave thee thus,
Aidless, alone, and smitten thro' the helm.
A little thing may harm a wounded man.
Yet I thy hest will all perform at full,
Watch what I see, and lightly bring thee word.'

So saying, from the ruin'd shrine he stept
And in the moon athwart the place of tombs,
Where lay the mighty bones of ancient men,
Old knights, and over them the sea-wind sang
Shrill, chill, with flakes of foam. He, stepping down
By zigzag paths, and juts of pointed rock,
Came on the shining levels of the lake.

There drew he forth the brand Excalibur,
And o'er him, drawing it, the winter moon,
Brightening the skirts of a long cloud, ran forth
And sparkled keen with frost against the hilt:
For all the haft twinkled with diamond sparks,
Myriads of topaz-lights, and jacinth-work

Of subtlest jewellery. He gazed so long
That both his eyes were dazzled, as he stood,
This way and that dividing the swift mind,
In act to throw: but at the last it seem'd
Better to leave Excalibur conceal'd
There in the many-knotted waterflags,
That whistled stiff and dry about the marge.
So strode he back slow to the wounded King.

    Then spake King Arthur to Sir Bedivere:
'Hast thou perform'd my mission which I gave?
What is it thou hast seen? or what hast heard?'

    And answer made the bold Sir Bedivere:
'I heard the ripple washing in the reeds,
And the wild water lapping on the crag.'

    To whom replied King Arthur, faint and pale:
'Thou hast betray'd thy nature and thy name,
Not rendering true answer, as beseem'd
Thy fealty, nor like a noble knight:
For surer sign had follow'd, either hand,
Or voice, or else a motion of the mere.
This is a shameful thing for men to lie.
Yet now, I charge thee, quickly go again
As thou art lief and dear, and do the thing
I bade thee, watch, and lightly bring me word.'

    Then went Sir Bedivere the second time
Across the ridge, and paced beside the mere,
Counting the dewy pebbles, fixed in thought;

But when he saw the wonder of the hilt,
How curiously and strangely chased, he smote
His palms together, and he cried aloud,

    'And if indeed I cast the brand away,
Surely a precious thing, one worthy note,
Should thus be lost forever from the earth,
Which might have pleased the eyes of many men.
What good should follow this, if this were done?
What harm, undone? deep harm to disobey,
Seeing obedience is the bond of rule.
Were it well to obey then, if a king demand
An act unprofitable, against himself?
The King is sick, and knows not what he does.
What record, or what relic of my lord
Should be to aftertime, but empty breath
And rumours of a doubt? but were this kept,
Stored in some treasure-house of mighty kings,
Some one might show it at a joust of arms,
Saying, 'King Arthur's sword, Excalibur,
Wrought by the lonely maiden of the Lake.
Nine years she wrought it, sitting in the deeps
Upon the hidden bases of the hills.'
So might some old man speak in the aftertime
To all the people, winning reverence.
But now much honour and much fame were lost.'

    So spake he, clouded with his own conceit,
And hid Excalibur the second time,
And so strode back slow to the wounded King.

  Then spoke King Arthur, breathing heavily:
'What is it thou hast seen, or what hast heard?'
  And answer made the bold Sir Bedivere:
'I heard the water lapping on the crag,
And the long ripple washing in the reeds.'

  To whom replied King Arthur, much in wrath:
'Ah, miserable and unkind, untrue,
Unknightly, traitor-hearted! Woe is me!
Authority forgets a dying king,
Laid widow'd of the power in his eye
That bow'd the will. I see thee what thou art,
For thou, the latest-left of all my knights,
In whom should meet the offices of all,
Thou wouldst betray me for the precious hilt;
Either from lust of gold, or like a girl
Valuing the giddy pleasure of the eyes.
Yet, for a man may fail in duty twice,
And the third time may prosper, get thee hence:
But, if thou spare to fling Excalibur,
I will arise and slay thee with my hands.'

  Then quickly rose Sir Bedivere, and ran,
And, leaping down the ridges lightly, plunged
Among the bulrush-beds, and clutch'd the sword,
And strongly wheel'd and threw it. The great brand
Made lightnings in the splendour of the moon,
And flashing round and round, and whirl'd in an arch,
Shot like a streamer of the northern morn,
Seen where the moving isles of winter shock
By night, with noises of the northern sea.
So flash'd and fell the brand Excalibur:

But ere he dipt the surface, rose an arm
Clothed in white samite, mystic, wonderful,
And caught him by the hilt, and brandish'd him
Three times, and drew him under in the mere.
And lightly went the other to the King.

Then spoke King Arthur, drawing thicker breath:
'Now see I by thine eyes that this is done.
Speak out: what is it thou hast heard, or seen?'

And answer made the bold Sir Bedivere:
'Sir King, I closed mine eyelids, lest the gems
Should blind my purpose, for I never saw,
Nor shall see, here or elsewhere, till I die,
Not tho' I live three lives of mortal men,
So great a miracle as yonder hilt.
Then with both hands I flung him, wheeling him;
But when I look'd again, behold an arm,
Clothed in white samite, mystic, wonderful,
That caught him by the hilt, and brandish'd him
Three times, and drew him under in the mere.'

And answer made King Arthur, breathing hard:
'My end draws nigh; 'tis time that I were gone.
Make broad thy shoulders to receive my weight,
And bear me to the margin; yet I fear
My wound hath taken cold, and I shall die.'

So saying, from the pavement he half rose,
Slowly, with pain, reclining on his arm,
And looking wistfully with wide blue eyes
As in a picture. Him Sir Bedivere

Remorsefully regarded thro' his tears,
And would have spoken, but he found not words,
Then took with care, and kneeling on one knee,
O'er both his shoulders drew the languid hands,
And rising bore him thro' the place of tombs.

    But, as he walk'd, King Arthur panted hard,
Like one that feels a nightmare on his bed
When all the house is mute. So sigh'd the King
Muttering and murmuring at his ear, 'Quick, quick!
I fear it is too late, and I shall die.'
But the other swiftly strode from ridge to ridge,
Clothed with his breath, and looking, as he walk'd
Larger than human on the frozen hills.
He heard the deep behind him, and a cry
Before. His own thought drove him like a goad.
Dry clash'd his harness in the icy caves
And barren chasms, and all to left and right
The bare black cliff clang'd round him, as he based
His feet on juts of slippery crag that rang
Sharp-smitten with the dint of armed heels –
And on a sudden, lo! the level lake,
And the long glories of the winter moon.

    Then saw they how there hove a dusky barge
Dark as a funeral scarf from stem to stern,
Beneath them; and descending they were ware
That all the decks were dense with stately forms
Black-stoled, black-hooded, like a dream – by these
Three Queens with crowns of gold – and from them rose
A cry that shiver'd to the tingling stars,

And, as it were one voice, an agony
Of lamentation, like a wind, that shrills
All night in a waste land, where no one comes,
Or hath come, since the making of the world.

    Then murmur'd Arthur, 'Place me in the barge,'
And to the barge they came. There those three Queens
Put forth their hands, and took the King, and wept.
But she that rose the tallest of them all
And fairest, laid his head upon her lap,
And loosed the shatter'd casque, and chafed his hands,
And call'd him by his name, complaining loud
And dropping bitter tears against his brow
Striped with dark blood: for all his face was white
And colourless, and like the wither'd moon
Smote by the fresh beam of the springing east;
And all his greaves and cuisses dash'd with drops
Of onset; and the light and lustrous curls –
That made his forehead like a rising sun
High from the daïs-throne – were parch'd with dust;
Or, clotted into points and hanging loose,
Mix'd with the knightly growth that fringed his lips.
So like a shatter'd column lay the King;
Not like that Arthur who, with lance in rest,
From spur to plume a star of tournament,
Shot thro' the lists at Camelot, and charged
Before the eyes of ladies and of kings.

    Then loudly cried the bold Sir Bedivere:
'Ah! my Lord Arthur, whither shall I go?
Where shall I hide my forehead and my eyes?
For now I see the true old times are dead,

When every morning brought a noble chance,
And every chance brought out a noble knight.
Such times have been not since the light that led
The holy Elders with the gift of myrrh.
But now the whole ROUND TABLE is dissolved
Which was an image of the mighty world;
And I, the last, go forth companionless,
And the days darken round me, and the years,
Among new men, strange faces, other minds.'

    And slowly answer'd Arthur from the barge:
'The old order changeth, yielding place to new,
And God fulfils Himself in many ways,
Lest one good custom should corrupt the world.
Comfort thyself: what comfort is in me?
I have lived my life, and that which I have done
May He within Himself make pure! but thou,
If thou shouldst never see my face again,
Pray for my soul. More things are wrought by prayer
Than this world dreams of. Wherefore, let thy voice
Rise like a fountain for me night and day.
For what are men better than sheep or goats
That nourish a blind life within the brain,
If, knowing God, they lift not hands of prayer
Both for themselves and those who call them friend?
For so the whole round earth is every way
Bound by gold chains about the feet of God.
But now farewell. I am going a long way
With these thou seëst – if indeed I go –
(For all my mind is clouded with a doubt)
To the island-valley of Avilion;
Where falls not hail, or rain, or any snow,

Nor ever wind blows loudly; but it lies
Deep-meadow'd, happy, fair with orchard-lawns
And bowery hollows crown'd with summer sea,
Where I will heal me of my grievous wound.'

    So said he, and the barge with oar and sail
Moved from the brink, like some full-breasted swan
That, fluting a wild carol ere her death,
Ruffles her pure cold plume, and takes the flood
With swarthy webs. Long stood Sir Bedivere
Revolving many memories, till the hull
Look'd one black dot against the verge of dawn,
And on the mere the wailing died away.

Break, Break, Break

Break, break, break,
 On thy cold gray stones, O Sea!
And I would that my tongue could utter
 The thoughts that arise in me.

O, well for the fisherman's boy,
 That he shouts with his sister at play!
O, well for the sailor lad,
 That he sings in his boat on the bay!

And the stately ships go on
 To their haven under the hill;
But O for the touch of a vanish'd hand,
 And the sound of a voice that is still!

Break, break, break
 At the foot of thy crags, O Sea!
But the tender grace of a day that is dead
 Will never come back to me.

St Agnes' Eve

Deep on the convent-roof the snows
    Are sparkling to the moon:
My breath to heaven like vapour goes;
    May my soul follow soon!
The shadows of the convent-towers
    Slant down the snowy sward,
Still creeping with the creeping hours
    That lead me to my Lord:
Make Thou my spirit pure and clear
    As are the frosty skies,
Or this first snowdrop of the year
    That in my bosom lies.

As these white robes are soil'd and dark,
    To yonder shining ground;
As this pale taper's earthly spark,
    To yonder argent round;
So shows my soul before the Lamb,
    My spirit before Thee;
So in mine earthly house I am,
    To that I hope to be.
Break up the heavens, O Lord! and far,
    Thro' all yon starlight keen,
Draw me, thy bride, a glittering star,
    In raiment white and clean.

He lifts me to the golden doors;
    The flashes come and go;
All heaven bursts her starry floors,
    And strews her lights below,

And deepens on and up! the gates
    Roll back, and far within
For me the Heavenly Bridegroom waits,
    To make me pure of sin.
The sabbaths of Eternity,
    One sabbath deep and wide –
A light upon the shining sea –
    The Bridegroom with his bride!

Locksley Hall

Comrades, leave me here a little, while as yet 'tis early morn:
Leave me here, and when you want me, sound upon the bugle-horn.

'Tis the place, and all around it, as of old, the curlews call,
Dreary gleams about the moorland flying over Locksley Hall;

Locksley Hall, that in the distance overlooks the sandy tracts,
And the hollow ocean-ridges roaring into cataracts.

Many a night from yonder ivied casement, ere I went to rest,
Did I look on great Orion sloping slowly to the West.

Many a night I saw the Pleiads, rising thro' the mellow shade,
Glitter like a swarm of fire-flies tangled in a silver braid.

Here about the beach I wander'd, nourishing a youth sublime
With the fairy tales of science, and the long result of Time;

When the centuries behind me like a fruitful land reposed;
When I clung to all the present for the promise that it closed:

When I dipt into the future far as human eye could see;
Saw the Vision of the world and all the wonder that
would be. –

In the Spring a fuller crimson comes upon the robin's
breast;
In the Spring the wanton lapwing gets himself another
crest;

In the Spring a livelier iris changes on the burnish'd dove;
In the Spring a young man's fancy lightly turns to
thoughts of love.

Then her cheek was pale and thinner than should be for
one so young,
And her eyes on all my motions with a mute observance
hung.

And I said, 'My cousin Amy, speak, and speak the truth to
me,
Trust me, cousin, all the current of my being sets to thee.'

On her pallid cheek and forehead came a colour and a
light,
As I have seen the rosy red flushing in the northern night.
And she turn'd – her bosom shaken with a sudden storm
of sighs –
All the spirit deeply dawning in the dark of hazel eyes –

Saying, 'I have hid my feelings, fearing they should do me
wrong;'
Saying, 'Dost thou love me, cousin?' weeping, 'I have
loved thee long.'

Love took up the glass of Time, and turn'd it in his
   glowing hands;
Every moment, lightly shaken, ran itself in golden sands.

Love took up the harp of Life, and smote on all the
   chords with might;
Smote the chord of Self, that, trembling, pass'd in music
   out of sight.

Many a morning on the moorland did we hear the copses
   ring,
And her whisper throng'd my pulses with the fulness of
   the Spring.

Many an evening by the waters did we watch the stately
   ships,
And our spirits rush'd together at the touching of the lips.

O my cousin, shallow-hearted! O my Amy, mine no
   more!
O the dreary, dreary moorland! O the barren, barren
   shore!

Falser than all fancy fathoms, falser than all songs have
   sung,
Puppet to a father's threat, and servile to a shrewish
   tongue!

Is it well to wish thee happy? – having known me – to
   decline
On a range of lower feelings and a narrower heart than
   mine!

Yet it shall be; thou shalt lower to his level day by day,
What is fine within thee growing coarse to sympathise
   with clay.

As the husband is, the wife is: thou art mated with a
   clown,
And the grossness of his nature will have weight to drag
   thee down.

He will hold thee, when his passion shall have spent its
   novel force,
Something better than his dog, a little dearer than his
   horse.

What is this? his eyes are heavy; think not they are glazed
   with wine.
Go to him: it is thy duty: kiss him: take his hand in
   thine.

It may be my lord is weary, that his brain is overwrought:
Soothe him with thy finer fancies, touch him with thy
   lighter thought.

He will answer to the purpose, easy things to
   understand –
Better thou wert dead before me, tho' I slew thee with
   my hand!

Better thou and I were lying, hidden from the heart's
   disgrace,
Roll'd in one another's arms, and silent in a last
   embrace.

Cursed be the social wants that sin against the strength of youth!
Cursed be the social lies that warp us from the living truth!

Cursed be the sickly forms that err from honest Nature's rule!
Cursed be the gold that gilds the straiten'd forehead of the fool!

Well – 'tis well that I should bluster! – Hadst thou less unworthy proved –
Would to God – for I had loved thee more than ever wife was loved.

Am I mad, that I should cherish that which bears but bitter fruit?
I will pluck it from my bosom, tho' my heart be at the root.

Never, tho' my mortal summers to such length of years should come
As the many-winter'd crow that leads the clanging rookery home.

Where is comfort? in division of the records of the mind?
Can I part her from herself, and love her, as I knew her, kind?

I remember one that perish'd; sweetly did she speak and move;
Such a one do I remember, whom to look at was to love.

Can I think of her as dead, and love her for the love she bore?
No — she never loved me truly; love is love for evermore.

Comfort? comfort scorn'd of devils! this is truth the poet sings,
That a sorrow's crown of sorrow is remembering happier things.

Drug thy memories, lest thou learn it, lest thy heart be put to proof,
In the dead unhappy night, and when the rain is on the roof.

Like a dog, he hunts in dreams, and thou art staring at the wall,
Where the dying night-lamp flickers, and the shadows rise and fall.

Then a hand shall pass before thee, pointing to his drunken sleep,
To thy widow'd marriage-pillows, to the tears that thou wilt weep.

Thou shalt hear the 'Never, never,' whisper'd by the phantom years,
And a song from out the distance in the ringing of thine ears;

And an eye shall vex thee, looking ancient kindness on thy pain.
Turn thee, turn thee on thy pillow; get thee to thy rest again.

Nay, but Nature brings thee solace; for a tender voice will cry.
'Tis a purer life than thine, a lip to drain thy trouble dry.

Baby lips will laugh me down; my latest rival brings thee rest.
Baby fingers, waxen touches, press me from the mother's breast.

O, the child too clothes the father with a dearness not his due.
Half is thine and half is his: it will be worthy of the two.

O, I see thee old and formal, fitted to thy petty part,
With a little hoard of maxims preaching down a daughter's heart.

'They were dangerous guides the feelings – she herself was not exempt –
Truly, she herself had suffer'd' – Perish in thy self-contempt!

Overlive it – lower yet – be happy! wherefore should I care?
I myself must mix with action, lest I wither by despair.

What is that which I should turn to, lighting upon days like these?
Every door is barr'd with gold, and opens but to golden keys.

Every gate is throng'd with suitors, all the markets overflow.
I have but an angry fancy: what is that which I should do?

I had been content to perish, falling on the foeman's
  ground,
When the ranks are roll'd in vapour, and the winds are
  laid with sound.

But the jingling of the guinea helps the hurt that Honour
  feels,
And the nations do but murmur, snarling at each other's
  heels.

Can I but relive in sadness? I will turn that earlier page.
Hide me from my deep emotion, O thou wondrous
  Mother-Age!

Make me feel the wild pulsation that I felt before the
  strife,
When I heard my days before me, and the tumult of my
  life;

Yearning for the large excitement that the coming years
  would yield,
Eager-hearted as a boy when first he leaves his father's
  field,

And at night along the dusky highway near and nearer
  drawn,
Sees in heaven the light of London flaring like a dreary
  dawn;

And his spirit leaps within him to be gone before him
  then,
Underneath the light he looks at, in among the throngs of
  men:

Men, my brothers, men the workers, ever reaping something new:
That which they have done but earnest of the things that they shall do:

For I dipt into the future, far as human eye could see,
Saw the Vision of the world, and all the wonder that would be;

Saw the heavens fill with commerce, argosies of magic sails,
Pilots of the purple twilight dropping down with costly bales;

Heard the heavens fill with shouting, and there rain'd a ghastly dew
From the nations' airy navies grappling in the central blue;

Far along the world-wide whisper of the south-wind rushing warm,
With the standards of the peoples plunging thro' the thunder-storm;

Till the war-drum throbb'd no longer, and the battle-flags were furl'd
In the Parliament of man, the Federation of the world.

There the common sense of most shall hold a fretful realm in awe,
And the kindly earth shall slumber, lapt in universal law.

So I triumph'd ere my passion sweeping thro' me left me dry,
Left me with the palsied heart, and left me with the jaundiced eye;

Eye, to which all order festers, all things here are out of joint:
Science moves, but slowly, slowly, creeping on from point to point:

Slowly comes a hungry people, as a lion, creeping nigher,
Glares at one that nods and winks behind a slowly-dying fire.

Yet I doubt not thro' the ages one increasing purpose runs,
And the thoughts of men are widen'd with the process of the suns.

What is that to him that reaps not harvest of his youthful joys,
Tho' the deep heart of existence beat for ever like a boy's?

Knowledge comes, but wisdom lingers, and I linger on the shore,
And the individual withers, and the world is more and more.

Knowledge comes, but wisdom lingers, and he bears a laden breast,
Full of sad experience, moving toward the stillness of his rest.

Hark, my merry comrades call me, sounding on the
   bugle-horn,
They to whom my foolish passion were a target for their
   scorn:

Shall it not be scorn to me to harp on such a moulder'd
   string?
I am shamed thro' all my nature to have loved so slight a
   thing.

Weakness to be wroth with weakness! woman's pleasure,
   woman's pain –
Nature made them blinder motions bounded in a
   shalower brain:

Woman is the lesser man, and all thy passions, match'd
   with mine,
Are as moonlight unto sunlight, and as water unto wine –

Here at least, where nature sickens, nothing. Ah, for some
   retreat
Deep in yonder shining Orient, where my life began to beat;

Where in wild Mahratta-battle fell my father evil-starr'd; –
I was left a trampled orphan, and a selfish uncle's ward.

Or to burst all links of habit – there to wander far away,
On from island unto island at the gateways of the day.

Larger constellations burning, mellow moons and happy
   skies,
Breadths of tropic shade and palms in cluster, knots of
   Paradise.

Never comes the trader, never floats an European
 flag,
Slides the bird o'er lustrous woodland, swings the trailer
 from the crag;

Droops the heavy-blossom'd bower, hangs the heavy-
 fruited tree –
Summer isles of Eden lying in dark-purple spheres of sea.

There methinks would be enjoyment more than in this
 march of mind,
In the steamship, in the railway, in the thoughts that shake
 mankind.

There the passions cramp'd no longer shall have scope
 and breathing space;
I will take some savage woman, she shall rear my dusky
 race.

Iron-jointed, supple-sinew'd, they shall dive, and they
 shall run,
Catch the wild goat by the hair, and hurl their lances in
 the sun;

Whistle back the parrot's call, and leap the rainbows of
 the brooks,
Not with blinded eyesight poring over miserable books –

Fool, again the dream, the fancy! but I know my words are
 wild,
But I count the gray barbarian lower than the Christian
 child.

I, to herd with narrow foreheads, vacant of our glorious
   gains,
Like a beast with lower pleasures, like a beast with lower
   pains!

Mated with a squalid savage – what to me were sun or
   clime?
I the heir of all the ages, in the foremost files of time –

I that rather held it better men should perish one by
   one,
Than that earth should stand at gaze like Joshua's moon in
   Ajalon!

Not in vain the distance beacons. Forward, forward let us
   range,
Let the great world spin for ever down the ringing
   grooves of change.

Thro' the shadow of the globe we sweep into the younger
   day;
Better fifty years of Europe than a cycle of Cathay.

Mother-Age (for mine I knew not) help me as when life
   begun:
Rift the hills, and roll the waters, flash the lightnings,
   weigh the Sun.

O, I see the crescent promise of my spirit hath not set.
Ancient founts of inspiration well thro' all my fancy yet.

Howsoever these things be, a long farewell to Locksley Hall!
Now for me the woods may wither, now for me the roof-tree fall.

Comes a vapour from the margin, blackening over heath and holt,
Cramming all the blast before it, in its breast a thunderbolt.

Let it fall on Locksley Hall, with rain or hail, or fire or snow;
For the mighty wind arises, roaring seaward, and I go.

The Lady of Shalott (1842 revision)

Part I

On either side the river lie
Long fields of barley and of rye,
That clothe the wold and meet the sky;
And thro' the field the road runs by
    To many-tower'd Camelot;
And up and down the people go,
Gazing where the lilies blow
Round an island there below,
    The island of Shalott.

Willows whiten, aspens quiver,
Little breezes dusk and shiver
Thro' the wave that runs for ever
By the island in the river
    Flowing down to Camelot.
Four gray walls, and four gray towers,
Overlook a space of flowers,
And the silent isle imbowers
    The Lady of Shalott.

By the margin, willow-veil'd,
Slide the heavy barges trail'd
By slow horses; and unhail'd
The shallop flitteth silken-sail'd
    Skimming down to Camelot:
But who hath seen her wave her hand?
Or at the casement seen her stand?

Or is she known in all the land,
>   The Lady of Shalott?

Only reapers, reaping early
In among the bearded barley,
Hear a song that echoes cheerly
From the river winding clearly,
>   Down to tower'd Camelot:
And by the moon the reaper weary,
Piling sheaves in uplands airy,
Listening, whispers ''Tis the fairy
>   Lady of Shalott.'

Part II

There she weaves by night and day
A magic web with colours gay.
She has heard a whisper say,
A curse is on her if she stay
>   To look down to Camelot.
She knows not what the curse may be,
And so she weaveth steadily,
And little other care hath she,
>   The Lady of Shalott.

And moving thro' a mirror clear
That hangs before her all the year,
Shadows of the world appear.
There she sees the highway near
>   Winding down to Camelot:
There the river eddy whirls,
And there the surly village-churls,

And the red cloaks of market girls,
        Pass onward from Shalott.

Sometimes a troop of damsels glad,
An abbot on an ambling pad,
Sometimes a curly shepherd-lad,
Or long-hair'd page in crimson clad,
        Goes by to tower'd Camelot;
And sometimes thro' the mirror blue
The knights come riding two and two:
She hath no loyal knight and true,
        The Lady of Shalott.

But in her web she still delights
To weave the mirror's magic sights,
For often thro' the silent nights
A funeral, with plumes and lights
        And music, went to Camelot:
Or when the moon was overhead,
Came two young lovers lately wed:
'I am half sick of shadows,' said
        The Lady of Shalott.

Part III

A bow-shot from her bower-eaves,
He rode between the barley-sheaves,
The sun came dazzling thro' the leaves,
And flamed upon the brazen greaves
        Of bold Sir Lancelot.
A red-cross knight for ever kneel'd
To a lady in his shield,

That sparkled on the yellow field,
    Beside remote Shalott.

The gemmy bridle glitter'd free,
Like to some branch of stars we see
Hung in the golden Galaxy.
The bridle bells rang merrily
    As he rode down to Camelot:
And from his blazon'd baldric slung
A mighty silver bugle hung,
And as he rode his armour rung,
    Beside remote Shalott.

All in the blue unclouded weather
Thick-jewell'd shone the saddle-leather,
The helmet and the helmet-feather
Burn'd like one burning flame together,
    As he rode down to Camelot.
As often thro' the purple night,
Below the starry clusters bright,
Some bearded meteor, trailing light,
    Moves over still Shalott.

His broad clear brow in sunlight glow'd;
On burnish'd hooves his war-horse trode;
From underneath his helmet flow'd
His coal-black curls as on he rode,
    As he rode down to Camelot.
From the bank and from the river
He flash'd into the crystal mirror,
'Tirra lirra,' by the river
    Sang Sir Lancelot.

She left the web, she left the loom,
She made three paces thro' the room,
She saw the water-lily bloom,
She saw the helmet and the plume,
    She look'd down to Camelot.
Out flew the web and floated wide;
The mirror crack'd from side to side;
'The curse is come upon me,' cried
    The Lady of Shalott.

Part IV

In the stormy east-wind straining,
The pale yellow woods were waning,
The broad stream in his banks complaining,
Heavily the low sky raining
    Over tower'd Camelot;
Down she came and found a boat
Beneath a willow left afloat,
And round about the prow she wrote
    The Lady of Shalott.

And down the river's dim expanse
Like some bold seër in a trance,
Seeing all his own mischance –
With a glassy countenance
    Did she look to Camelot.
And at the closing of the day
She loosed the chain, and down she lay;
The broad stream bore her far away,
    The Lady of Shalott.

Lying, robed in snowy white
That loosely flew to left and right —
The leaves upon her falling light —
Thro' the noises of the night
      She floated down to Camelot:
And as the boat-head wound along
The willowy hills and fields among,
They heard her singing her last song,
      The Lady of Shalott.

Heard a carol, mournful, holy,
Chanted loudly, chanted lowly,
Till her blood was frozen slowly,
And her eyes were darken'd wholly,
      Turn'd to tower'd Camelot.
For ere she reach'd upon the tide
The first house by the water-side,
Singing in her song she died,
      The Lady of Shalott.

Under tower and balcony,
By garden-wall and gallery,
A gleaming shape she floated by,
Dead-pale between the houses high,
      Silent into Camelot.
Out upon the wharfs they came,
Knight and burgher, lord and dame,
And round the prow they read her name,
      The Lady of Shalott.

Who is this? and what is here?
And in the lighted palace near

Died the sound of royal cheer;
And they cross'd themselves for fear,
    All the knights at Camelot:
But Lancelot mused a little space;
He said, 'She has a lovely face;
God in his mercy lend her grace,
    The Lady of Shalott.'

Godiva

I waited for the train at Coventry;
I hung with grooms and porters on the bridge,
To watch the three tall spires; and there I shaped
The city's ancient legend into this: –

    Not only we, the latest seed of Time,
New men, that in the flying of a wheel
Cry down the past, not only we, that prate
Of rights and wrongs, have loved the people well,
And loathed to see them overtax'd; but she
Did more, and underwent, and overcame,
The woman of a thousand summers back,
Godiva, wife to that grim Earl, who ruled
In Coventry: for when he laid a tax
Upon his town, and all the mothers brought
Their children, clamouring, 'If we pay, we starve!'
She sought her lord, and found him, where he strode
About the hall, among his dogs, alone,
His beard a foot before him and his hair
A yard behind. She told him of their tears,
And pray'd him, 'If they pay this tax, they starve.'
Whereat he stared, replying, half-amazed,
'You would not let your little finger ache
For such as *these*?' – 'But I would die,' said she.
He laugh'd, and swore by Peter and by Paul;
Then fillip'd at the diamond in her ear;
'Oh ay, ay, ay, you talk!' – 'Alas!' she said,
'But prove me what I would not do.'
And from a heart as rough as Esau's hand,
He answer'd, 'Ride you naked thro' the town,
And I repeal it;' and nodding, as in scorn,

He parted, with great strides among his dogs.
    So left alone, the passions of her mind,
As winds from all the compass shift and blow,
Made war upon each other for an hour,
Till pity won. She sent a herald forth,
And bade him cry, with sound of trumpet, all
The hard condition; but that she would loose
The people: therefore, as they loved her well,
From then till noon no foot should pace the street,
No eye look down, she passing; but that all
Should keep within, door shut, and window barr'd.
    Then fled she to her inmost bower, and there
Unclasp'd the wedded eagles of her belt,
The grim Earl's gift; but ever at a breath
She linger'd, looking like a summer moon
Half-dipt in cloud: anon she shook her head,
And shower'd the rippled ringlets to her knee;
Unclad herself in haste; adown the stair
Stole on; and, like a creeping sunbeam, slid
From pillar unto pillar, until she reach'd
The gateway; there she found her palfrey trapt
In purple blazon'd with armorial gold.
    Then she rode forth, clothed on with chastity:
The deep air listen'd round her as she rode,
And all the low wind hardly breathed for fear.
The little wide-mouth'd heads upon the spout
Had cunning eyes to see: the barking cur
Made her cheek flame: her palfrey's footfall shot
Light horrors thro' her pulses: the blind walls
Were full of chinks and holes; and overhead
Fantastic gables, crowding, stared: but she
Not less thro' all bore up, till, last, she saw

The white-flower'd elder-thicket from the field,
Gleam thro' the Gothic archways in the wall.

    Then she rode back, clothed on with chastity:
And one low churl, compact of thankless earth,
The fatal byword of all years to come,
Boring a little auger-hole in fear,
Peep'd – but his eyes, before they had their will,
Were shrivel'd into darkness in his head,
And dropt before him. So the Powers, who wait
On noble deeds, cancell'd a sense misused;
And she, that knew not, pass'd: and all at once,
With twelve great shocks of sound, the shameless noon
Was clash'd and hammer'd from a hundred towers,
One after one: but even then she gain'd
Her bower; whence reissuing, robed and crown'd,
To meet her lord, she took the tax away
And built herself an everlasting name.

The Vision of Sin

I

I had a vision when the night was late:
A youth came riding toward a palace-gate.
He rode a horse with wings, that would have flown,
But that his heavy rider kept him down.
And from the palace came a child of sin,
And took him by the curls, and led him in,
Where sat a company with heated eyes,
Expecting when a fountain should arise:
A sleepy light upon their brows and lips —
As when the sun, a crescent of eclipse,
Dreams over lake and lawn, and isles and capes —
Suffused them, sitting, lying, languid shapes,
By heaps of gourds, and skins of wine, and piles of
    grapes.

II

Then methought I heard a mellow sound,
Gathering up from all the lower ground;
Narrowing in to where they sat assembled
Low voluptuous music winding trembled,
Wov'n in circles: they that heard it sigh'd,
Panted hand in hand with faces pale,
Swung themselves, and in low tones replied;
Till the fountain spouted, showering wide
Sleet of diamond-drift and pearly hail;
Then the music touch'd the gates and died;
Rose again from where it seem'd to fail,
Storm'd in orbs of song, a growing gale;
Till thronging in and in, to where they waited,

As 'twere a hundred-throated nightingale,
The strong tempestuous treble throbb'd and palpitated;
Ran into its giddiest whirl of sound,
Caught the sparkles, and in circles,
Purple gauzes, golden hazes, liquid mazes,
Flung the torrent rainbow round:
Then they started from their places,
Moved with violence, changed in hue,
Caught each other with wild grimaces,
Half-invisible to the view,
Wheeling with precipitate paces
To the melody, till they flew,
Hair, and eyes, and limbs, and faces,
Twisted hard in fierce embraces,
Like to Furies, like to Graces,
Dash'd together in blinding dew:
Till, kill'd with some luxurious agony,
The nerve-dissolving melody
Flutter'd headlong from the sky.

III

And then I look'd up toward a mountain-tract,
That girt the region with high cliff and lawn:
I saw that every morning, far withdrawn
Beyond the darkness and the cataract,
God made himself an awful rose of dawn,
Unheeded: and detaching, fold by fold,
From those still heights, and, slowly drawing near,
A vapour heavy, hueless, formless, cold,
Came floating on for many a month and year,
Unheeded: and I thought I would have spoken,
And warn'd that madman ere it grew too late:

But, as in dreams, I could not. Mine was broken,
When that cold vapour touch'd the palace-gate,
And link'd again. I saw within my head
A gray and gap-tooth'd man as lean as death,
Who slowly rode across a wither'd heath,
And lighted at a ruin'd inn, and said:

IV

'Wrinkled ostler, grim and thin!
    Here is custom come your way;
Take my brute, and lead him in,
    Stuff his ribs with mouldy hay.

'Bitter barmaid, waning fast!
    See that sheets are on my bed;
What! the flower of life is past:
    It is long before you wed.

'Slip-shod waiter, lank and sour,
    At the Dragon on the heath!
Let us have a quiet hour,
    Let us hob-and-nob with Death.

'I am old, but let me drink;
    Bring me spices, bring me wine;
I remember, when I think,
    That my youth was half divine.

'Wine is good for shrivell'd lips,
    When a blanket wraps the day,
When the rotten woodland drips,
    And the leaf is stamp'd in clay.

'Sit thee down, and have no shame,
   Cheek by jowl, and knee by knee:
What care I for any name?
   What for order or degree?

'Let me screw thee up a peg:
   Let me loose thy tongue with wine:
Callest thou that thing a leg?
   Which is thinnest? thine or mine?

'Thou shalt not be saved by works:
   Thou hast been a sinner too:
Ruin'd trunks on wither'd forks,
   Empty scarecrows, I and you!

'Fill the cup, and fill the can:
   Have a rouse before the morn:
Every moment dies a man,
   Every moment one is born.

'We are men of ruin'd blood;
   Therefore comes it we are wise.
Fish are we that love the mud,
   Rising to no fancy-flies.

'Name and fame! to fly sublime
   Thro' the courts, the camps, the schools,
Is to be the ball of Time,
   Bandied by the hands of fools.

'Friendship! – to be two in one –
   Let the canting liar pack!

Well I know, when I am gone,
   How she mouths behind my back.

'Virtue! – to be good and just –
   Every heart, when sifted well,
Is a clot of warmer dust,
   Mix'd with cunning sparks of hell.

'O! we two as well can look
   Whited thought and cleanly life
As the priest, above his book
   Leering at his neighbour's wife.

'Fill the cup, and fill the can:
   Have a rouse before the morn:
Every moment dies a man,
   Every moment one is born.

'Drink, and let the parties rave:
   They are fill'd with idle spleen;
Rising, falling, like a wave,
   For they know not what they mean.

'He that roars for liberty
   Faster binds a tyrant's power;
And the tyrant's cruel glee
   Forces on the freer hour.

'Fill the can, and fill the cup:
   All the windy ways of men
Are but dust that rises up,
   And is lightly laid again.

'Greet her with applausive breath,
    Freedom, gaily doth she tread;
In her right a civic wreath,
    In her left a human head.

'No, I love not what is new;
    She is of an ancient house:
And I think we know the hue
    Of that cap upon her brows.

'Let her go! her thirst she slakes
    Where the bloody conduit runs:
Then her sweetest meal she makes
    On the first-born of her sons.

'Drink to lofty hopes that cool
    Visions of a perfect State:
Drink we, last, the public fool,
    Frantic love and frantic hate.

'Chant me now some wicked stave,
    Till thy drooping courage rise,
And the glow-worm of the grave
    Glimmer in thy rheumy eyes.

'Fear not thou to loose thy tongue;
    Set thy hoary fancies free;
What is loathsome to the young
    Savours well to thee and me.

'Change, reverting to the years,
    When thy nerves could understand

What there is in loving tears,
    And the warmth of hand in hand.

'Tell me tales of thy first love
    April hopes, the fools of chance;
Till the graves begin to move,
    And the dead begin to dance.

'Fill the can, and fill the cup:
    All the windy ways of men
Are but dust that rises up,
    And is lightly laid again.

'Trooping from their mouldy dens
    The chap-fallen circle spreads:
Welcome, fellow-citizens,
    Hollow hearts and empty heads!

'You are bones, and what of that?
    Every face, however full,
Padded round with flesh and fat,
    Is but modell'd on a skull.

'Death is king, and Vivat Rex!
    Tread a measure on the stones,
Madam – if I know your sex,
    From the fashion of your bones.

'No, I cannot praise the fire
    In your eye – nor yet your lip:
All the more do I admire
    Joints of cunning workmanship.

'Lo! God's likeness – the ground-plan
   Neither modell'd, glazed, or framed:
Buss me, thou rough sketch of man,
   Far too naked to be shamed!

'Drink to Fortune, drink to Chance,
   While we keep a little breath!
Drink to heavy Ignorance!
   Hob-and-nob with brother Death!

'Thou art mazed, the night is long,
   And the longer night is near:
What! I am not all as wrong
   As a bitter jest is dear.

'Youthful hopes, by scores, to all,
   When the locks are crisp and curl'd;
Unto me my maudlin gall
   And my mockeries of the world.

'Fill the cup, and fill the can!
   Mingle madness, mingle scorn!
Dregs of life, and lees of man:
   Yet we will not die forlorn.'

V

The voice grew faint: there came a further change:
Once more uprose the mystic mountain-range:
Below were men and horses pierced with worms,
And slowly quickening into lower forms;
By shards and scurf of salt, and scum of dross,
Old plash of rains, and refuse patch'd with moss,

Then some one spake: 'Behold! it was a crime
Of sense avenged by sense that wore with time.'
Another said: 'The crime of sense became
The crime of malice, and is equal blame.'
And one: 'He had not wholly quench'd his power;
A little grain of conscience made him sour.'
At last I heard a voice upon the slope
Cry to the summit, 'Is there any hope?'
To which an answer peal'd from that high land,
But in a tongue no man could understand;
And on the glimmering limit far withdrawn
God made Himself an awful rose of dawn.

Lady Clara Vere de Vere

Lady Clara Vere de Vere,
    Of me you shall not win renown:
You thought to break a country heart
    For pastime, ere you went to town.
At me you smiled, but unbeguiled
    I saw the snare, and I retired;
The daughter of a hundred earls,
    You are not one to be desired.

Lady Clara Vere de Vere,
    I know you proud to bear your name;
Your pride is yet no mate for mine,
    Too proud to care from whence I came.
Nor would I break for your sweet sake
    A heart that dotes on truer charms.
A simple maiden in her flower
    Is worth a hundred coats-of-arms.

Lady Clara Vere de Vere,
    Some meeker pupil you must find,
For, were you queen of all that is,
    I could not stoop to such a mind.
You sought to prove how I could love,
    And my disdain is my reply.
The lion on your old stone gates
    Is not more cold to you than I.

Lady Clara Vere de Vere,
    You put strange memories in my head.
Not thrice your branching limes have blown

    Since I beheld young Laurence dead.
O, your sweet eyes, your low replies!
    A great enchantress you may be;
But there was that across his throat
    Which you had hardly cared to see.

Lady Clara Vere de Vere,
    When thus he met his mother's view,
She had the passion of her kind,
    She spake some certain truths of you.
Indeed I heard one bitter word
    That scarce is fit for you to hear;
Her manners had not that repose
    Which stamps the caste of Vere de Vere.

Lady Clara Vere de Vere,
    There stands a spectre in your hall;
The guilt of blood is at your door;
    You changed a wholesome heart to gall.
You held your course without remorse,
    To make him trust his modest worth,
And, last, you fix'd a vacant stare,
    And slew him with your noble birth.

Trust me, Clara Vere de Vere,
    From yon blue heavens above us bent
The gardener Adam and his wife
    Smile at the claims of long descent.
Howe'er it be, it seems to me,
    'Tis only noble to be good.
Kind hearts are more than coronets,
    And simple faith than Norman blood.

I know you, Clara Vere de Vere,
    You pine among your halls and towers;
The languid light of your proud eyes
    Is wearied of the rolling hours.
In glowing health, with boundless wealth,
    But sickening of a vague disease,
You know so ill to deal with time,
    You needs must play such pranks as these.

Clara, Clara Vere de Vere,
    If Time be heavy on your hands,
Are there no beggars at your gate,
    Nor any poor about your lands?
O, teach the orphan-boy to read,
    Or teach the orphan-girl to sew;
Pray Heaven for a human heart,
    And let the foolish yeoman go.

Tears, Idle Tears (from *The Princess*)

'Tears, idle tears, I know not what they mean,
Tears from the depth of some divine despair
Rise in the heart, and gather to the eyes,
In looking on the happy Autumn-fields,
And thinking of the days that are no more.

'Fresh as the first beam glittering on a sail,
That brings our friends up from the underworld,
Sad as the last which reddens over one
That sinks with all we love below the verge;
So sad, so fresh, the days that are no more.

'Ah, sad and strange as in dark summer dawns
The earliest pipe of half-awaken'd birds
To dying ears, when unto dying eyes
The casement slowly grows a glimmering square;
So sad, so strange, the days that are no more.

'Dear as remember'd kisses after death,
And sweet as those by hopeless fancy feign'd
On lips that are for others; deep as love,
Deep as first love, and wild with all regret;
O Death in Life, the days that are no more.'

Ask Me No More (from *The Princess*)

Ask me no more: the moon may draw the sea;
    The cloud may stoop from heaven and take shape
    With fold to fold, of mountain or of cape;
But O too fond, when have I answer'd thee?
        Ask me no more.

Ask me no more: what answer should I give?
    I love not hollow cheek or faded eye:
    Yet, O my friend, I will not have thee die!
Ask me no more, lest I should bid thee live;
        Ask me no more.

Ask me no more: thy fate and mine are seal'd:
    I strove against the stream and all in vain:
    Let the great river take me to the main:
No more, dear love, for at a touch I yield;
        Ask me no more.

Ring Out, Wild Bells (from *In Memoriam*)

Ring out, wild bells, to the wild sky,
    The flying cloud, the frosty light:
    The year is dying in the night;
Ring out, wild bells, and let him die.

Ring out the old, ring in the new,
    Ring, happy bells, across the snow:
    The year is going, let him go;
Ring out the false, ring in the true.

Ring out the grief that saps the mind
    For those that here we see no more;
    Ring out the feud of rich and poor,
Ring in redress to all mankind.

Ring out a slowly dying cause,
    And ancient forms of party strife;
    Ring in the nobler modes of life,
With sweeter manners, purer laws.

Ring out the want, the care, the sin,
    The faithless coldness of the times;
    Ring out, ring out my mournful rhymes
But ring the fuller minstrel in.

Ring out false pride in place and blood,
    The civic slander and the spite;
    Ring in the love of truth and right,
Ring in the common love of good.

Ring out old shapes of foul disease;
    Ring out the narrowing lust of gold;
    Ring out the thousand wars of old,
Ring in the thousand years of peace.

Ring in the valiant man and free,
    The larger heart, the kindlier hand;
    Ring out the darkness of the land,
Ring in the Christ that is to be.

I Envy Not in Any Moods (from *In Memoriam*)

I envy not in any moods
    The captive void of noble rage,
    The linnet born within the cage,
That never knew the summer woods:

I envy not the beast that takes
    His license in the field of time,
    Unfetter'd by the sense of crime,
To whom a conscience never wakes;

Nor, what may count itself as blest,
    The heart that never plighted troth
    But stagnates in the weeds of sloth;
Nor any want-begotten rest.

I hold it true, whate'er befall;
    I feel it, when I sorrow most;
    'Tis better to have loved and lost
Than never to have loved at all.

The Eagle

He clasps the crag with crooked hands;
Close to the sun in lonely lands,
Ring'd with the azure world, he stands.

The wrinkled sea beneath him crawls;
He watches from his mountain walls,
And like a thunderbolt he falls.

Ode on the Death of the Duke of Wellington

I

Bury the Great Duke
    With an empire's lamentation,
Let us bury the Great Duke
    To the noise of the mourning of a mighty nation,
Mourning when their leaders fall,
Warriors carry the warrior's pall,
And sorrow darkens hamlet and hall.

II

Where shall we lay the man whom we deplore?
Here, in streaming London's central roar.
Let the sound of those he wrought for,
And the feet of those he fought for,
Echo round his bones for evermore.

III

Lead out the pageant: sad and slow,
As fits an universal woe,
Let the long long procession go,
And let the sorrowing crowd about it grow,
And let the mournful martial music blow;
The last great Englishman is low.

IV

Mourn, for to us he seems the last,
Remembering all his greatness in the Past.
No more in soldier fashion will he greet
With lifted hand the gazer in the street.
O friends, our chief state-oracle is mute:

Mourn for the man of long-enduring blood,
The statesman-warrior, moderate, resolute,
Whole in himself, a common good.
Mourn for the man of amplest influence,
Yet clearest of ambitious crime,
Our greatest yet with least pretence,
Great in council and great in war,
Foremost captain of his time,
Rich in saving common-sense,
And, as the greatest only are,
In his simplicity sublime.
O good gray head which all men knew,
O voice from which their omens all men drew,
O iron nerve to true occasion true,
O fall'n at length that tower of strength
Which stood four-square to all the winds that blew!
Such was he whom we deplore.
The long self-sacrifice of life is o'er.
The great World-victor's victor will be seen no more.

V

All is over and done:
Render thanks to the Giver,
England, for thy son.
Let the bell be toll'd.
Render thanks to the Giver,
And render him to the mould.
Under the cross of gold
That shines over city and river,
There he shall rest for ever
Among the wise and the bold.
Let the bell be toll'd:

And a reverent people behold
The towering car, the sable steeds:
Bright let it be with its blazon'd deeds,
Dark in its funeral fold.
Let the bell be toll'd:
And a deeper knell in the heart be knoll'd;
And the sound of the sorrowing anthem roll'd
Thro' the dome of the golden cross;
And the volleying cannon thunder his loss;
He knew their voices of old.
For many a time in many a clime
His captain's-ear has heard them boom
Bellowing victory, bellowing doom:
When he with those deep voices wrought,
Guarding realms and kings from shame;
With those deep voices our dead captain taught
The tyrant, and asserts his claim
In that dread sound to the great name,
Which he has worn so pure of blame,
In praise and in dispraise the same,
A man of well-attemper'd frame.
O civic muse, to such a name,
To such a name for ages long,
To such a name,
Preserve a broad approach of fame,
And ever-echoing avenues of song.

VI

Who is he that cometh, like an honour'd guest,
With banner and with music, with soldier and with priest,
With a nation weeping, and breaking on my rest?

Mighty Seaman, this is he
Was great by land as thou by sea.
Thine island loves thee well, thou famous man,
The greatest sailor since our world began.
Now, to the roll of muffled drums,
To thee the greatest soldier comes;
For this is he
Was great by land as thou by sea;
His foes were thine; he kept us free;
O give him welcome, this is he
Worthy of our gorgeous rites,
And worthy to be laid by thee;
For this is England's greatest son,
He that gain'd a hundred fights,
Nor ever lost an English gun;
This is he that far away
Against the myriads of Assaye
Clash'd with his fiery few and won;
And underneath another sun,
Warring on a later day,
Round affrighted Lisbon drew
The treble works, the vast designs
Of his labour'd rampart lines,
Where he greatly stood at bay,
Whence he issued forth anew,
And ever great and greater grew,
Beating from the wasted vines
Back to France her banded swarms,
Back to France with countless blows,
Till o'er the hills her eagles flew
Beyond the Pyrenean pines,
Follow'd up in valley and glen

With blare of bugle, clamour of men,
Roll of cannon and clash of arms,
And England pouring on her foes.
Such a war had such a close.
Again their ravening eagle rose
In anger, wheel'd on Europe-shadowing wings,
And barking for the thrones of kings;
Till one that sought but Duty's iron crown
On that loud sabbath shook the spoiler down;
A day of onsets of despair!
Dash'd on every rocky square
Their surging charges foam'd themselves away;
Last, the Prussian trumpet blew;
Thro' the long-tormented air
Heaven flash'd a sudden jubilant ray,
And down we swept and charged and over-threw.
So great a soldier taught us there,
What long-enduring hearts could do
In that world-earthquake, Waterloo!
Mighty Seaman, tender and true,
And pure as he from taint of craven guile,
O saviour of the silver-coasted isle,
O shaker of the Baltic and the Nile,
If aught of things that here befall
Touch a spirit among things divine,
If love of country move thee there at all,
Be glad, because his bones are laid by thine!
And thro' the centuries let a people's voice
In full acclaim,
A people's voice,
The proof and echo of all human fame,
A people's voice, when they rejoice

At civic revel and pomp and game,
Attest their great commander's claim
With honour, honour, honour, honour to him,
Eternal honour to his name.

VII

A people's voice! we are a people yet.
Tho' all men else their nobler dreams forget,
Confus'd by brainless mobs and lawless Powers;
Thank Him who isl'd us here, and roughly set
His Briton in blown seas and storming showers,
We have a voice, with which to pay the debt
Of boundless love and reverence and regret
To those great men who fought, and kept it ours.
And keep it ours, O God, from brute control;
O Statesmen, guard us, guard the eye, the soul
Of Europe, keep our noble England whole,
And save the one true seed of freedom sown
Betwixt a people and their ancient throne,
That sober freedom out of which there springs
Our loyal passion for our temperate kings;
For, saving that, ye help to save mankind
Till public wrong be crumbled into dust,
And drill the raw world for the march of mind,
Till crowds at length be sane and crowns be just.
But wink no more in slothful overtrust.
Remember him who led your hosts;
He bade you guard the sacred coasts.
Your cannons moulder on the seaward wall;
His voice is silent in your council-hall
For ever; and whatever tempests lour
For ever silent; even if they broke

In thunder, silent; yet remember all
He spoke among you, and the Man who spoke;
Who never sold the truth to serve the hour,
Nor palter'd with Eternal God for power;
Who let the turbid streams of rumour flow
Thro' either babbling world of high and low;
Whose life was work, whose language rife
With rugged maxims hewn from life;
Who never spoke against a foe;
Whose eighty winters freeze with one rebuke
All great self-seekers trampling on the right:
Truth-teller was our England's Alfred nam'd;
Truth-lover was our English Duke;
Whatever record leap to light
He never shall be shamed.

VIII

Lo, the leader in these glorious wars
Now to glorious burial slowly borne,
Follow'd by the brave of other lands,
He, on whom from both her open hands
Lavish Honour shower'd all her stars,
And affluent Fortune emptied all her horn.
Yea, let all good things await
Him who cares not to be great,
But as he saves or serves the state.
Not once or twice in our rough island-story,
The path of duty was the way to glory:
He that walks it, only thirsting
For the right, and learns to deaden
Love of self, before his journey closes,
He shall find the stubborn thistle bursting

Into glossy purples, which outredden
All voluptuous garden-roses.
Not once or twice in our fair island-story,
The path of duty was the way to glory:
He, that ever following her commands,
On with toil of heart and knees and hands,
Thro' the long gorge to the far light has won
His path upward, and prevail'd,
Shall find the toppling crags of Duty scal'd
Are close upon the shining table-lands
To which our God Himself is moon and sun.
Such was he: his work is done.
But while the races of mankind endure,
Let his great example stand
Colossal, seen of every land,
And keep the soldier firm, the statesman pure:
Till in all lands and thro' all human story
The path of duty be the way to glory:
And let the land whose hearths he sav'd from shame
For many and many an age proclaim
At civic revel and pomp and game,
And when the long-illumined cities flame,
Their ever-loyal iron leader's fame,
With honour, honour, honour, honour to him,
Eternal honour to his name.

IX

Peace, his triumph will be sung
By some yet unmoulded tongue
Far on in summers that we shall not see:
Peace, it is a day of pain
For one about whose patriarchal knee

Late the little children clung:
O peace, it is a day of pain
For one, upon whose hand and heart and brain
Once the weight and fate of Europe hung.
Ours the pain, be his the gain!
More than is of man's degree
Must be with us, watching here
At this, our great solemnity.
Whom we see not we revere;
We revere, and we refrain
From talk of battles loud and vain,
And brawling memories all too free
For such a wise humility
As befits a solemn fane:
We revere, and while we hear
The tides of Music's golden sea
Setting toward eternity,
Uplifted high in heart and hope are we,
Until we doubt not that for one so true
There must be other nobler work to do
Than when he fought at Waterloo,
And victor he must ever be.
For tho' the Giant Ages heave the hill
And break the shore, and evermore
Make and break, and work their will;
Tho' world on world in myriad myriads roll
Round us, each with different powers,
And other forms of life than ours,
What know we greater than the soul?
On God and Godlike men we build our trust.
Hush, the Dead March wails in the people's ears:

The dark crowd moves, and there are sobs and tears:
The black earth yawns: the mortal disappears;
Ashes to ashes, dust to dust;
He is gone who seem'd so great. –
Gone; but nothing can bereave him
Of the force he made his own
Being here, and we believe him
Something far advanced in State,
And that he wears a truer crown
Than any wreath that man can weave him.
Speak no more of his renown,
Lay your earthly fancies down,
And in the vast cathedral leave him,
God accept him, Christ receive him.

The Charge of the Light Brigade

I

Half a league, half a league,
    Half a league onward,
All in the valley of Death
    Rode the six hundred.
'Forward, the Light Brigade!
Charge for the guns!' he said.
Into the valley of Death
    Rode the six hundred.

II

'Forward, the Light Brigade!'
Was there a man dismay'd?
Not though the soldier knew
    Someone had blunder'd.
Theirs not to make reply,
Theirs not to reason why,
Theirs but to do and die.
Into the valley of Death
    Rode the six hundred.

III

Cannon to right of them,
Cannon to left of them,
Cannon in front of them
    Volley'd and thunder'd;

Stormed at with shot and shell,
Boldly they rode and well,
Into the jaws of Death,
Into the mouth of Hell
    Rode the six hundred.

IV

Flash'd all their sabres bare,
Flash'd as they turned in air
Sabring the gunners there,
Charging an army, while
    All the world wonder'd.
Plunged in the battery-smoke
Right through the line they broke;
Cossack and Russian
Reel'd from the sabre stroke
    Shatter'd and sunder'd.
Then they rode back, but not
    Not the six hundred.

V

Cannon to right of them,
Cannon to left of them,
Cannon behind them
    Volley'd and thunder'd;
Storm'd at with shot and shell,
While horse and hero fell.
They that had fought so well
Came thro' the jaws of Death,

Back from the mouth of Hell,
All that was left of them,
    Left of six hundred.

VI

When can their glory fade?
O the wild charge they made!
    All the world wonder'd.
Honour the charge they made!
Honour the Light Brigade,
    Noble six hundred!

Come into the Garden, Maud (from *Maud*)

A Monodrama

Come into the garden, Maud,
    For the black bat, night, has flown,
Come into the garden, Maud,
    I am here at the gate alone;
And the woodbine spices are wafted abroad,
    And the musk of the rose is blown.

For a breeze of morning moves,
    And the planet of Love is on high,
Beginning to faint in the light that she loves
    In a bed of daffodil sky,
To faint in the light of the sun she loves,
    To faint in his light, and to die.

All night have the roses heard
    The flute, violin, bassoon;
All night has the casement jessamine stirr'd
    To the dancers dancing in tune;
Till a silence fell with the waking bird,
    And a hush with the setting moon.

I said to the lily, 'There is but one
    With whom she has heart to be gay.
When will the dancers leave her alone?
    She is weary of dance and play.'
Now half to the setting moon are gone,
    And half to the rising day;

Low on the sand and loud on the stone
    The last wheel echoes away.

I said to the rose, 'The brief night goes
    In babble and revel and wine.
O young lord-lover, what sighs are those,
    For one that will never be thine?
But mine, but mine,' so I sware to the rose,
    'For ever and ever, mine.'

And the soul of the rose went into my blood,
    As the music clash'd in the hall;
And long by the garden lake I stood,
    For I heard your rivulet fall
From the lake to the meadow and on to the wood,
    Our wood, that is dearer than all;

From the meadow your walks have left so sweet
    That whenever a March-wind sighs
He sets the jewel-print of your feet
    In violets blue as your eyes,
To the woody hollows in which we meet
    And the valleys of Paradise.

The slender acacia would not shake
    One long milk-bloom on the tree;
The white lake-blossom fell into the lake
    As the pimpernel dozed on the lea;
But the rose was awake all night for your sake,
    Knowing your promise to me;
The lilies and roses were all awake,
    They sigh'd for the dawn and thee.

Queen rose of the rosebud garden of girls,
    Come hither, the dances are done,
In gloss of satin and glimmer of pearls,
    Queen lily and rose in one;
Shine out, little head, sunning over with curls,
    To the flowers, and be their sun.

There has fallen a splendid tear
    From the passion-flower at the gate.
She is coming, my dove, my dear;
    She is coming, my life, my fate;
The red rose cries, 'She is near, she is near;'
    And the white rose weeps, 'She is late;'
The larkspur listens, 'I hear, I hear;'
    And the lily whispers, 'I wait.'

She is coming, my own, my sweet;
    Were it ever so airy a tread,
My heart would hear her and beat,
    Were it earth in an earthy bed;
My dust would hear her and beat,
    Had I lain for a century dead;
Would start and tremble under her feet,
    And blossom in purple and red.

The War

There is a sound of thunder afar,
    Storm in the South that darkens the day,
Storm of battle and thunder of war,
    Well, if it do not roll our way.
        Form! form! Riflemen form!
        Ready, be ready to meet the storm!
        Riflemen, riflemen, riflemen form!

Be not deaf to the sound that warns!
    Be not gull'd by a despot's plea!
Are figs of thistles, or grapes of thorns?
    How should a despot set men free?
        Form! form! Riflemen form!
        Ready, be ready to meet the storm!
        Riflemen, riflemen, riflemen form!

Let your Reforms for a moment go,
    Look to your butts and take good aims.
Better a rotten borough or so,
    Than a rotten fleet or city in flames!
        Form! form! Riflemen form!
        Ready, be ready to meet the storm!
        Riflemen, riflemen, riflemen form!

Form, be ready to do or die!
    Form in Freedom's name and Queen's!
True, that we have a faithful ally,
    But only the devil knows what he means.
        Form! form! Riflemen form!
        Ready, be ready to meet the storm!
        Riflemen, riflemen, riflemen form!

Tithonus

The woods decay, the woods decay and fall,
The vapours weep their burthen to the ground,
Man comes and tills the field and lies beneath,
And after many a summer dies the swan.
Me only cruel immortality
Consumes: I wither slowly in thine arms,
Here at the quiet limit of the world,
A white-hair'd shadow roaming like a dream
The ever-silent spaces of the East,
Far-folded mists, and gleaming halls of morn.

Alas! for this gray shadow, once a man –
So glorious in his beauty and thy choice,
Who madest him thy chosen, that he seem'd
To his great heart none other than a God!
I ask'd thee, 'Give me immortality.'
Then didst thou grant mine asking with a smile,
Like wealthy men, who care not how they give.
But thy strong Hours indignant work'd their wills,
And beat me down and marr'd and wasted me,
And tho' they could not end me, left me maim'd
To dwell in presence of immortal youth,
Immortal age beside immortal youth,
And all I was, in ashes. Can thy love,
Thy beauty, make amends, tho' even now,
Close over us, the silver star, thy guide,
Shines in those tremulous eyes that fill with tears
To hear me? Let me go: take back thy gift:
Why should a man desire in any way
To vary from the kindly race of men,

Or pass beyond the goal of ordinance
Where all should pause, as is most meet for all?

    A soft air fans the cloud apart; there comes
A glimpse of that dark world where I was born.
Once more the old mysterious glimmer steals
From thy pure brows, and from thy shoulders pure,
And bosom beating with a heart renew'd.
Thy cheek begins to redden thro' the gloom,
Thy sweet eyes brighten slowly close to mine,
Ere yet they blind the stars, and the wild team
Which love thee, yearning for thy yoke, arise,
And shake the darkness from their loosen'd manes,
And beat the twilight into flakes of fire.

    Lo! ever thus thou growest beautiful
In silence, then before thine answer given
Departest, and thy tears are on my cheek.

    Why wilt thou ever scare me with thy tears,
And make me tremble lest a saying learnt,
In days far-off, on that dark earth, be true?
'The Gods themselves cannot recall their gifts.'

    Ay me! ay me! with what another heart
In days far-off, and with what other eyes
I used to watch — if I be he that watch'd —
The lucid outline forming round thee; saw
The dim curls kindle into sunny rings;
Changed with thy mystic change, and felt my blood
Glow with the glow that slowly crimson'd all
Thy presence and thy portals, while I lay,

Mouth, forehead, eyelids, growing dewy-warm
With kisses balmier than half-opening buds
Of April, and could hear the lips that kiss'd
Whispering I knew not what of wild and sweet,
Like that strange song I heard Apollo sing,
While Ilion like a mist rose into towers.

    Yet hold me not for ever in thine East:
How can my nature longer mix with thine?
Coldly thy rosy shadows bathe me, cold
Are all thy lights, and cold my wrinkled feet
Upon thy glimmering thresholds, when the steam
Floats up from those dim fields about the homes
Of happy men that have the power to die,
And grassy barrows of the happier dead.
Release me, and restore me to the ground;
Thou seëst all things, thou wilt see my grave:
Thou wilt renew thy beauty morn by morn;
I earth in earth forget these empty courts,
And thee returning on thy silver wheels.

Song from the Marriage of Geraint
(from *Idylls of the King*)

    Turn, Fortune, turn thy wheel, and lower the proud;
Turn thy wild wheel thro' sunshine, storm, and cloud;
Thy wheel and thee we neither love nor hate.

    Turn, Fortune, turn thy wheel with smile or frown;
With that wild wheel we go not up or down;
Our hoard is little, but our hearts are great.

    Smile and we smile, the lords of many lands;
Frown and we smile, the lords of our own hands;
For man is man and master of his fate.

    Turn, turn thy wheel above the staring crowd;
Thy wheel and thou are shadows in the cloud;
Thy wheel and thee we neither love nor hate.

In the Valley of Cauteretz

All along the valley, stream that flashest white,
Deepening thy voice with the deepening of the night,
All along the valley, where thy waters flow,
I walk'd with one I loved two and thirty years ago.
All along the valley, while I walk'd to-day,
The two and thirty years were a mist that rolls away;
For all along the valley, down thy rocky bed,
Thy living voice to me was as the voice of the dead,
And all along the valley, by rock and cave and tree,
The voice of the dead was a living voice to me.

Northern Farmer (Old Style)

Wheer 'asta beän saw long and meä liggin' 'ere aloän?
Noorse? thoort nowt o' a noorse: whoy, Doctor's abeän
   an' agoän:
Says that I moänt 'a naw moor aäle: but I beänt a fool:
Git ma my aäle, fur I beänt a-gawin' to breäk my rule.

Doctors, they knaws nowt, fur a says what's nawways true:
Naw soort o' koind o' use to saäy the things that a do.
I've 'ed my point o' aäle ivry noight sin' I beän 'ere,
An' I've 'ed my quart ivry market-noight for foorty year.

Parson's a beän loikewoise, an' a sittin' 'ere o' my bed.
'The amoighty's a taäkin o' you to 'issén, my friend,' a
   said,
An' a towd ma my sins, an's toithe were due, an' I gied it
   in hond;
I done moy duty boy 'um, as I 'a done boy the lond.

Larn'd a ma' beä. I reckons I 'annot sa mooch to larn.
But a cast oop, thot a did, 'bout Bessy Marris's barne.
Thaw a knaws I hallus voäted wi' Squoire an' choorch an'
   staäte,
An' i' the woost o' toimes I wur niver agin the raäte.

An' I hallus coom'd to 's choorch afoor moy Sally wur
   deäd,
An' 'eard 'um a bummin' awaäy loike a buzzard-clock
   ower me 'eäd,

An' I niver knaw'd whot a meän'd but I thowt a 'ad
  summut to saäy,
An' I thowt a said what a owt to 'a said an' I coom'd
  awaäy.

Bessy Marris's barne! tha knaws she laäid it to meä.
Mowt a beän, mayhap, for she wur a bad un, sheä.
'Siver, I kep 'um, I kep 'um, my lass, tha mun under-
  stond;
I done moy duty boy 'um as I 'a done boy the lond.

But Parson a cooms an' a goäs, an' a says it easy an'
  freeä:
'The amoighty's taäkin o' you to 'issén, my friend,'
  says 'eä.
I weänt saäy men be loiars, thaw summun said it in
  'aäste:
But 'e reäds wonn sarmin a weeäk, an' I 'a stubb'd
  Thurnaby waäste.

D'ya moind the waäste, my lass? naw, naw, tha was not
  born then;
Theer wur a boggle in it, I often 'eärd 'um mysén;
Moäst loike a butter-bump, fur I 'eärd 'um about an'
  about,
But I stubb'd 'um oop wi' the lot, an' raäved an' rembled
  'um out.

Keäper's it wur; fo' they fun 'um theer a-laäid of 'is faäce
Down i' the woild 'enemies afoor I coom'd to the plaäce.

Noäks or Thimbleby – toäner 'ed shot 'um as dead as a
   naäil.
Noäks wur 'ang'd for it oop at 'soize – but git ma my
   aäle.

Dubbut looök at the waäaste: theer warn't not feeäd for a
   cow;
Nowt at all but bracken an' fuzz, an' looök at it now –
Warn't worth nowt a haäcre, an' now theer's lots o' feeäd,
Fourscoor yows upon it, an' some on it down i' seeäd.

Nobbut a bit on it's left, an' I meän'd to 'a stubb'd it at
   fall,
Done it ta-year I meän'd, an' runn'd plow thruff it an' all,
If godamoighty an' parson 'ud nobbut let ma aloän,
Meä, wi' haäte hoonderd haäcre o' Squoire's, an' lond o'
   my oän.

Do godamoighty knaw what a's doing a-taäkin' o' meä?
I beänt wonn as saws 'ere a beän an' yonder a peä;
An' Squoire 'ull be sa mad an' all – a' dear, a' dear!
And I 'a managed for Squoire coom Michaelmas thutty
   year.

A mowt 'a taäen owd Joänes, as 'ant not a 'aäpoth o'
   sense,
Or a mowt 'a taäen young Robins – a niver mended a
   fence:
But godamoighty a moost taäke meä an' taäke ma now
Wi' aäf the cows to cauve an' Thurnaby hoälms to plow!

Loook 'ow quoloty smoiles when they seeäs ma a passin'
   boy,
Says to thessén, naw doubt, 'What a man a beä sewer-loy!'
Fur they knaws what I beän to Squoire sin' fust a coom'd
   to the 'All;
I done moy duty by Squoire an' I done moy duty boy
   hall.

Squoire 's i' Lunnon, an' summun I reckons 'ull 'a to
   wroite,
For whoä's to howd the lond ater meä that muddles ma
   quoit;
Sartin-sewer I beä, thot a weänt niver give it to Joänes,
Naw, nor a moänt to Robins – a niver rembles the stoäns.

But summun 'ull come ater meä mayhap wi' 'is kittle o'
   steäm
Huzzin' an' maazin' the blessed feälds wi' the Divil's oän
   teäm.
Sin' I mun doy I mun doy, thaw loife they says is sweet,
But sin' I mun doy I mun doy, for I couldn abeär to see
   it.

What atta stannin' theer fur, an' doesn bring me the aäle?
Doctor's a 'toättler, lass, an a's hallus i' the owd taäle;
I weänt breäk rules fur Doctor, a knaws naw moor nor a
   floy;
Git ma my aäle, I tell tha, an' if I mun doy I mun doy.

Northern Farmer (New Style)

Dosn't thou 'ear my 'erse's legs, as they canters awaäy?
Proputty, proputty, proputty — that's what I 'ears 'em
  saäy.
Proputty, proputty, proputty — Sam, thou's an ass for thy
  paaïns:
Theer's moor sense i' one o' 'is legs, nor in all thy
  braaïns.

Woä — theer's a craw to pluck wi' tha, Sam: yon's parson's
  'ouse —
Dosn't thou knaw that a man mun be eäther a man or a
  mouse?
Time to think on it then; for thou'll be twenty to weeäk.
Proputty, proputty — woä then, woä — let ma 'ear mysén
  speäk.

Me an' thy muther, Sammy, 'as been a-talkin' o' thee;
Thou's beän talkin' to muther, an' she beän a tellin' it me.
Thou'll not marry for munny — thou's sweet upo' parson's
  lass —
Noä — thou'll marry for luvv — an' we boäth of us thinks
  tha an ass.

Seeä'd her todaäy goä by — Saäint's-daäy — they was
  ringing the bells.
She's a beauty thou thinks — an' soä is scoors o' gells,
Them as 'as munny an' all — wot's a beauty? — the flower
  as blaws.
But proputty, proputty sticks, an' proputty, proputty graws.

Do'ant be stunt: taäke time: I knaws what maäkes tha sa mad.
Warn't I craäzed fur the lasses mysén when I wur a lad?
But I knaw'd a Quaäker feller as often 'as towd ma this:
'Doänt thou marry for munny, but goä wheer munny is!'

An' I went wheer munny war; an' thy muther coom to 'and,
Wi' lots o' munny laaïd by, an' a nicetish bit o' land.
Maäybe she warn't a beauty – I niver giv it a thowt –
But warn't she as good to cuddle an' kiss as a lass as 'ant nowt?

Parson's lass 'ant nowt, an' she weänt 'a nowt when 'e's deäd,
Mun be a guvness, lad, or summut, and addle her breäd.
Why? for 'e's nobbut a curate, an' weänt niver get hissen clear,
An' 'e maäde the bed as 'e ligs on afoor 'e coom'd to the shere.

An' thin 'e coom'd to the parish wi' lots o' Varsity debt,
Stook to his taäil thy did, an' 'e 'ant got shut on 'em yet.
An' 'e ligs on 'is back i' the grip, wi' noän to lend 'im a shuvv,
Woorse nor a far-welter'd yowe: fur, Sammy, 'e married for luvv.

Luvv? what's luvv? thou can luvv thy lass an' 'er munny too,
Maäkin' 'em goä togither, as they've good right to do.

Could'n I luvv thy muther by cause o' 'er munny laaïd
  by?
Naäy – fur I luvv'd 'er a vast sight moor fur it: reäson
  why.

Ay, an' thy muther says thou wants to marry the lass,
Cooms of a gentleman burn: an' we boäth on us thinks
  tha an ass.
Woä then, proputty, wiltha? – an ass as near as mays
  nowt –
Woä then, wiltha? dangtha! – the bees is as fell as owt.

Breäk me a bit o' the esh for his 'eäd, lad, out o' the
  fence!
Gentleman burn! what's gentleman burn? is it shillins an'
  pence?
Proputty, proputty's ivrything 'ere, an', Sammy, I'm blest
If it isn't the saäme oop yonder, fur them as 'as it's the
  best.

Tis'n them as 'as munny as breaks into 'ouses an' steäls,
Them as 'as coats to their backs an' taäkes their regular
  meäls,
Noä, but it's them as niver knaws wheer a meäl's to be
  'ad.
Taäke my word for it Sammy, the poor in a loomp is
  bad.

Them or thir feythers, tha sees, mun 'a beän a laäzy lot,
Fur work mun 'a gone to the gittin' whiniver munny was
  got.

Feyther 'ad ammost nowt; leastways 'is munny was 'id.
But 'e tued an' moil'd issén dead, an' 'e died a good un,
   'e did.

Looök thou theer wheer Wrigglesby beck cooms out by
   the 'ill!
Feyther run oop to the farm, an' I runs oop to the mill;
An' I'll run oop to the brig, an' that thou'll live to see;
And if thou marries a good un I'll leäve the land to thee.

Thim's my noätions, Sammy, wheerby I means to stick;
But if thou marries a bad un, I'll leäve the land to
   Dick. –
Coom oop, proputty, proputty – that's what I 'ears 'im
   saäy –
Proputty, proputty, proputty – canter an' canter awaäy.

Lucretius

Lucilia, wedded to Lucretius, found
Her master cold; for when the morning flush
Of passion and the first embrace had died
Between them, tho' he lov'd her none the less,
Yet often when the woman heard his foot
Return from pacings in the field, and ran
To greet him with a kiss, the master took
Small notice, or austerely, for – his mind
Half buried in some weightier argument,
Or fancy-borne perhaps upon the rise
And long roll of the Hexameter – he past
To turn and ponder those three hundred scrolls
Left by the Teacher, whom he held divine.
She brook'd it not; but wrathful, petulant,
Dreaming some rival, sought and found a witch
Who brew'd the philtre which had power, they said,
To lead an errant passion home again.
And this, at times, she mingled with his drink,
And this destroy'd him; for the wicked broth
Confused the chemic labour of the blood.
And tickling the brute brain within the man's
Made havock among those tender cells, and check'd
His power to shape: he loathed himself; and once
After a tempest woke upon a morn
That mock'd him with returning calm, and cried:

    'Storm in the night! for thrice I heard the rain
Rushing; and once the flash of a thunderbolt –
Methought I never saw so fierce a fork –
Struck out the streaming mountain-side, and show'd

A riotous confluence of watercourses
Blanching and billowing in a hollow of it,
Where all but yester-eve was dusty-dry.

    'Storm, and what dreams, ye holy Gods, what
        dreams!
For thrice I waken'd after dreams. Perchance
We do but recollect the dreams that come
Just ere the waking: terrible! for it seem'd
A void was made in Nature; all her bonds
Crack'd; and I saw the flaring atom-streams
And torrents of her myriad universe,
Ruining along the illimitable inane,
Fly on to clash together again, and make
Another and another frame of things
For ever: that was mine, my dream, I knew it —
Of and belonging to me, as the dog
With inward yelp and restless forefoot plies
His function of the woodland: but the next!
I thought that all the blood by Sylla shed
Came driving rainlike down again on earth,
And where it dash'd the reddening meadow, sprang
No dragon warriors from Cadmean teeth,
For these I thought my dream would show to me,
But girls, Hetairai, curious in their art,
Hired animalisms, vile as those that made
The mulberry-faced Dictator's orgies worse
Than aught they fable of the quiet Gods.
And hands they mixt, and yell'd and round me drove
In narrowing circles till I yell'd again
Half-suffocated, and sprang up, and saw —
Was it the first beam of my latest day?

'Then, then, from utter gloom stood out the breasts,
The breasts of Helen, and hoveringly a sword
Now over and now under, now direct,
Pointed itself to pierce, but sank down shamed
At all that beauty; and as I stared, a fire,
The fire that left a roofless Ilion,
Shot out of them, and scorch'd me that I woke.

'Is this thy vengeance, holy Venus, thine,
Because I would not one of thine own doves,
Not ev'n a rose, were offer'd to thee? thine,
Forgetful how my rich prooemion makes
Thy glory fly along the Italian field,
In lays that will outlast thy Deity?

'Deity? nay, thy worshippers. My tongue
Trips, or I speak profanely. Which of these
Angers thee most, or angers thee at all?
Not if thou be'st of those who, far aloof
From envy, hate and pity, and spite and scorn,
Live the great life which all our greatest fain
Would follow, centre'd in eternal calm.

'Nay, if thou canst, O Goddess, like ourselves
Touch, and be touch'd, then would I cry to thee
To kiss thy Mavors, roll thy tender arms
Round him, and keep him from the lust of blood
That makes a steaming slaughter-house of Rome.

'Ay, but I meant not thee; I meant not her,
Whom all the pines of Ida shook to see
Slide from that quiet heaven of hers, and tempt

The Trojan, while his neat-herds were abroad;
Nor her that o'er her wounded hunter wept
Her Deity false in human-amorous tears;
Nor whom her beardless apple-arbiter
Decided fairest. Rather, O ye Gods,
Poet-like, as the great Sicilian called
Calliope to grace his golden verse –
Ay, and this Kypris also – did I take
That popular name of thine to shadow forth
The all-generating powers and genial heat
Of Nature, when she strikes thro' the thick blood
Of cattle, and light is large, and lambs are glad
Nosing the mother's udder, and the bird
Makes his heart voice amid the blaze of flowers:
Which things appear the work of mighty Gods.

   'The Gods! and if I go my work is left
Unfinish'd – if I go. The Gods, who haunt
The lucid interspace of world and world,
Where never creeps a cloud, or moves a wind,
Nor ever falls the least white star of snow,
Nor ever lowest roll of thunder moans,
Nor sound of human sorrow mounts to mar
Their sacred everlasting calm! and such,
Not all so fine, nor so divine a calm,
Not such, nor all unlike it, man may gain
Letting his own life go. The Gods, the Gods!
If all be atoms, how then should the Gods
Being atomic not be dissoluble,
Not follow the great law? My master held
That Gods there are, for all men so believe.
I prest my footsteps into his, and meant

Surely to lead my Memmius in a train
Of flowery clauses onward to the proof
That Gods there are, and deathless. Meant? I meant?
I have forgotten what I meant: my mind
Stumbles, and all my faculties are lamed.

   'Look where another of our Gods, the Sun,
Apollo, Delius, or of older use
All-seeing Hyperion – what you will –
Has mounted yonder; since he never sware,
Except his wrath were wreak'd on wretched man,
That he would only shine among the dead
Hereafter; tales! for never yet on earth
Could dead flesh creep, or bits of roasting ox
Moan round the spit – nor knows he what he sees;
King of the East altho' he seem, and girt
With song and flame and fragrance, slowly lifts
His golden feet on those empurpled stairs
That climb into the windy halls of heaven:
And here he glances on an eye new-born,
And gets for greeting but a wail of pain;
And here he stays upon a freezing orb
That fain would gaze upon him to the last;
And here upon a yellow eyelid fall'n
And closed by those who mourn a friend in vain,
Not thankful that his troubles are no more.
And me, altho' his fire is on my face
Blinding, he sees not, nor at all can tell
Whether I mean this day to end myself,
Or lend an ear to Plato where he says,
That men like soldiers may not quit the post
Allotted by the Gods: but he that holds

The Gods are careless, wherefore need he care
Greatly for them, nor rather plunge at once,
Being troubled, wholly out of sight, and sink
Past earthquake – ay, and gout and stone, that break
Body toward death, and palsy, death-in-life,
And wretched age – and worst disease of all,
These prodigies of myriad nakednesses,
And twisted shapes of lust, unspeakable,
Abominable, strangers at my hearth
Not welcome, harpies miring every dish,
The phantom husks of something foully done,
And fleeting thro' the boundless universe,
And blasting the long quiet of my breast
With animal heat and dire insanity?

    'How should the mind, except it loved them, clasp
These idols to herself? or do they fly
Now thinner, and now thicker, like the flakes
In a fall of snow, and so press in, perforce
Of multitude, as crowds that in an hour
Of civic tumult jam the doors, and bear
The keepers down, and throng, their rags and they
The basest, far into that council-hall
Where sit the best and stateliest of the land?

    'Can I not fling this horror off me again,
Seeing with how great ease Nature can smile,
Balmier and nobler from her bath of storm,
At random ravage? and how easily
The mountain there has cast his cloudy slough,
Now towering o'er him in serenest air,

A mountain o'er a mountain, — ay, and within
All hollow as the hopes and fears of men?

    'But who was he, that in the garden snared
Picus and Faunus, rustic Gods? a tale
To laugh at — more to laugh at in myself —
For look! what is it? there? yon arbutus
Totters; a noiseless riot underneath
Strikes through the wood, sets all the tops quivering —
The mountain quickens into Nymph and Faun;
And here an Oread — how the sun delights
To glance and shift about her slippery sides,
And rosy knees and supple roundedness,
And budded bosom-peaks — who this way runs
Before the rest — A satyr, a satyr, see,
Follows; but him I proved impossible;
Twy-natured is no nature: yet he draws
Nearer and nearer, and I scan him now
Beastlier than any phantom of his kind
That ever butted his rough brother-brute
For lust or lusty blood or provender:
I hate, abhor, spit, sicken at him; and she
Loathes him as well; such a precipitate heel,
Fledged as it were with Mercury's ankle-wing,
Whirls her to me: but will she fling herself,
Shameless upon me? Catch her, goat-foot: nay,
Hide, hide them, million-myrtled wilderness,
And cavern-shadowing laurels, hide! do I wish —
What? — that the bush were leafless? or to whelm
All of them in one massacre? O ye Gods,
I know you careless, yet, behold, to you
From childly wont and ancient use I call —

I thought I lived securely as yourselves –
No lewdness, narrowing envy, monkey-spite,
No madness of ambition, avarice, none:
No larger feast than under plane or pine
With neighbours laid along the grass, to take
Only such cups as left us friendly-warm,
Affirming each his own philosophy –
Nothing to mar the sober majesties
Of settled, sweet, Epicurean life.
But now it seems some unseen monster lays
His vast and filthy hands upon my will,
Wrenching it backward into his; and spoils
My bliss in being; and it was not great;
For save when shutting reasons up in rhythm,
Or Heliconian honey in living words,
To make a truth less harsh, I often grew
Tired of so much within our little life,
Or of so little in our little life –
Poor little life that toddles half an hour
Crown'd with a flower or two, and there an end –
And since the nobler pleasure seems to fade,
Why should I, beastlike as I find myself,
Not manlike end myself? – our privilege –
What beast has heart to do it? And what man,
What Roman would be dragg'd in triumph thus?
Not I; not he, who bears one name with her
Whose death-blow struck the dateless doom of
   kings,
When, brooking not the Tarquin in her veins,
She made her blood in sight of Collatine
And all his peers, flushing the guiltless air,
Spout from the maiden fountain in her heart.

And from it sprang the Commonwealth, which breaks
As I am breaking now!
                    'And therefore now
Let her, that is the womb and tomb of all,
Great Nature, take, and forcing far apart
Those blind beginnings that have made me man,
Dash them anew together at her will
Thro' all her cycles – into man once more,
Or beast or bird or fish, or opulent flower:
But till this cosmic order everywhere
Shatter'd into one earthquake in one day
Cracks all to pieces, – and that hour perhaps
Is not so far when momentary man
Shall seem no more a something to himself,
But he, his hopes and hates, his homes and fanes,
And even his bones long laid within the grave,
The very sides of the grave itself shall pass,
Vanishing, atom and void, atom and void,
Into the unseen for ever, – till that hour,
My golden work in which I told a truth
That stays the rolling Ixionian wheel,
That numbs the Fury's ringlet-snake, and plucks
The mortal soul from out immortal hell,
Shall stand: ay, surely: then it fails at last
And perishes as I must; for O Thou,
Passionless bride, divine Tranquillity,
Yearn'd after by the wisest of the wise,
Who fail to find thee, being as thou art
Without one pleasure and without one pain,
Howbeit I know thou surely must be mine
Or soon or late, yet out of season, thus
I woo thee roughly, for thou carest not

How roughly men may woo thee so they win —
Thus — thus: the soul flies out and dies in the air.'

    With that he drove the knife into his side:
She heard him raging, heard him fall; ran in,
Beat breast, tore hair, cried out upon herself
As having fail'd in duty to him, shriek'd
That she but meant to win him back, fell on him,
Clasp'd, kiss'd him, wail'd: he answer'd, 'Care not thou!
The duty? What is duty Fare thee well!'

Marriage Morning

Light, so low upon earth,
    You send a flash to the sun.
Here is the golden close of love,
    All my wooing is done.
Oh, all the woods and the meadows,
    Woods, where we hid from the wet,
Stiles where we stayed to be kind,
    Meadows in which we met!
Light, so low in the vale
    You flash and lighten afar,
For this is the golden morning of love,
    And you are his morning star.
Flash, I am coming, I come,
    By meadow and stile and wood,
Oh, lighten into my eyes and my heart,
    Into my heart and my blood!
Heart, are you great enough
    For a love that never tires?
O heart, are you great enough for love?
    I have heard of thorns and briers.
Over the thorns and briers,
    Over the meadows and stiles,
Over the world to the end of it
    Flash for a million miles.

Tiresias

I wish I were as in the years of old,
While yet the blessed daylight made itself
Ruddy thro' both the roofs of sight, and woke
These eyes, now dull, but then so keen to seek
The meanings ambush'd under all they saw,
The flight of birds, the flame of sacrifice,
What omens may foreshadow fate to man
And woman, and the secret of the Gods.

     My son, the Gods, despite of human prayer,
Are slower to forgive than human kings.
The great God, Arês, burns in anger still
Against the guiltless heirs of him from Tyre,
Our Cadmus, out of whom thou art, who found
Beside the springs of Dircê, smote, and still'd
Thro' all its folds the multitudinous beast
The dragon, which our trembling fathers call'd
The God's own son.

              A tale, that told to me,
When but thine age, by age as winter-white
As mine is now, amazed, but made me yearn
For larger glimpses of that more than man
Which rolls the heavens, and lifts, and lays the deep,
Yet loves and hates with mortal hates and loves,
And moves unseen among the ways of men.

     Then, in my wanderings all the lands that lie
Subjected to the Heliconian ridge
Have heard this footstep fall, altho' my wont
Was more to scale the highest of the heights
With some strange hope to see the nearer God.

     One naked peak – the sister of the sun

Would climb from out the dark, and linger there
To silver all the valleys with her shafts –
There once, but long ago, five-fold thy term
Of years, I lay; the winds were dead for heat;
The noonday crag made the hand burn; and sick
For shadow – not one bush was near – I rose
Following a torrent till its myriad falls
Found silence in the hollows underneath.

    There in a secret olive-glade I saw
Pallas Athene climbing from the bath
In anger; yet one glittering foot disturb'd
The lucid well; one snowy knee was prest
Against the margin flowers; a dreadful light
Came from her golden hair, her golden helm
And all her golden armour on the grass,
And from her virgin breast, and virgin eyes
Remaining fixt on mine, till mine grew dark
For ever, and I heard a voice that said
'Henceforth be blind, for thou hast seen too much,
And speak the truth that no man may believe.'

    Son, in the hidden world of sight that lives
Behind this darkness, I behold her still,
Beyond all work of those who carve the stone,
Beyond all dreams of Godlike womanhood,
Ineffable beauty, out of whom, at a glance
And as it were, perforce, upon me flash'd
The power of prophesying – but to me
No power – so chain'd and coupled with the curse
Of blindness and their unbelief, who heard
And heard not, when I spake of famine, plague,
Shrine-shattering earthquake, fire, flood, thunderbolt,
And angers of the Gods for evil done

And expiation lack'd – no power on Fate,
Theirs, or mine own! for when the crowd would roar
For blood, for war, whose issue was their doom,
To cast wise words among the multitude
Was flinging fruit to lions; nor, in hours
Of civil outbreak, when I knew the twain
Would each waste each, and bring on both the yoke
Of stronger states, was mine the voice to curb
The madness of our cities and their kings.

  Who ever turn'd upon his heel to hear
My warning that the tyranny of one
Was prelude to the tyranny of all?
My counsel that the tyranny of all
Led backward to the tyranny of one?

  This power hath work'd no good to aught that lives,
And these blind hands were useless in their wars.
O therefore, that the unfulfill'd desire,
The grief for ever born from griefs to be
The boundless yearning of the Prophet's heart –
Could *that* stand forth, and like a statue, rear'd
To some great citizen, win all praise from all
Who past it, saying, 'That was he!'
         In vain!
Virtue must shape itself in deed, and those
Whom weakness or necessity have cramp'd
Within themselves, immerging, each, his urn
In his own well, draws solace as he may.

  Menaceus, thou hast eyes, and I can hear
Too plainly what full tides of onset sap
Our seven high gates, and what a weight of war
Rides on those ringing axles! jingle of bits,
Shouts, arrows, tramp of the hornfooted horse

That grind the glebe to powder! Stony showers
Of that ear-stunning hail of Arês crash
Along the sounding walls. Above, below,
Shock after shock, the song-built towers and gates
Reel, bruised and butted with the shuddering
War-thunder of iron rams; and from within
The city comes a murmur void of joy,
Lest she be taken captive – maidens, wives,
And mothers with their babblers of the dawn,
And oldest age in shadow from the night,
Falling about their shrines before their Gods,
And wailing, 'Save us.'
                      And they wail to thee!
These eyeless eyes, that cannot see thine own,
See this, that only in thy virtue lies
The saving of our Thebes; for, yesternight,
To me, the great God Arês, whose one bliss
Is war and human sacrifice – himself
Blood-red from battle, spear and helmet tipt
With stormy light as on a mast at sea,
Stood out before a darkness, crying, 'Thebes,
Thy Thebes shall fall and perish, for I loathe
The seed of Cadmus – yet if one of these
By his own hand – if one of these –'
                                       My son,
No sound is breathed so potent to coerce,
And to conciliate, as their names who dare
For that sweet mother land which gave them birth
Nobly to do, nobly to die. Their names,
Graven on memorial columns, are a song
Heard in the future; few, but more than wall
And rampart, their examples reach a hand

Far thro' all years, and everywhere they meet
And kindle generous purpose, and the strength
To mould it into action pure as theirs.

     Fairer thy fate than mine, if life's best end
Be to end well! and thou refusing this,
Unvenerable will thy memory be
While men shall move the lips; but if thou dare –
Thou, one of these, the race of Cadmus – then
No stone is fitted in yon marble girth
Whose echo shall not tongue thy glorious doom,
Nor in this pavement but shall ring thy name
To every hoof that clangs it, and the springs
Of Dircê laving yonder battle-plain,
Heard from the roofs by night, will murmur thee
To thine own Thebes, while Thebes thro' thee shall stand
Firm-based with all her Gods.

     The Dragon's cave
Half hid, they tell me, now in flowing vines –
Where once he dwelt and whence he roll'd himself
At dead of night – thou knowest, and that smooth rock
Before it, altar-fashion'd, where of late
The woman-breasted Sphinx, with wings drawn back,
Folded her lion paws, and look'd to Thebes.
There blanch the bones of whom she slew, and these
Mixt with her own, because the fierce beast found
A wiser than herself, and dash'd herself
Dead in her rage: but thou art wise enough,
Tho' young, to love thy wiser, blunt the curse
Of Pallas, hear, and tho' I speak the truth
Believe I speak it, let thine own hand strike
Thy youthful pulses into rest and quench
The red God's anger, fearing not to plunge

Thy torch of life in darkness, rather – thou
Rejoicing that the sun, the moon, the stars
Send no such light upon the ways of men
As one great deed.
      Thither, my son, and there
Thou, that hast never known the embrace of love,
Offer thy maiden life.
      This useless hand!
I felt one warm tear fall upon it. Gone!
He will achieve his greatness.
      But for me,
I would that I were gather'd to my rest,
And mingled with the famous kings of old
On whom about their ocean-islets flash
The faces of the Gods – the wise man's word,
Here trampled by the populace underfoot
There crown'd with worship – and these eyes will find
The men I knew, and watch the chariot whirl
About the goal again, and hunters race
The shadowy lion, and the warrior-kings,
In height and prowess more than human, strive
Again for glory, while the golden lyre
Is ever sounding in heroic ears
Heroic hymns, and every way the vales
Wind, clouded with the grateful incense-fume
Of those who mix all odour to the Gods
On one far height in one far-shining fire.

The Ancient Sage

A thousand summers ere the time of Christ
From out his ancient city came a Seer
Whom one that loved, and honour'd him, and yet
Was no disciple, richly garb'd, but worn
From wasteful living, follow'd – in his hand
A scroll of verse – till that old man before
A cavern whence an affluent fountain pour'd
From darkness into daylight, turn'd and spoke.

This wealth of waters might but seem to draw
From yon dark cave, but, son, the source is higher,
Yon summit half-a-league in air – and higher,
The cloud that hides it – higher still, the heavens
Whereby the cloud was moulded, and whereout
The cloud descended. Force is from the heights.
I am wearied of our city, son, and go
To spend my one last year among the hills.
What hast thou there? Some deathsong for the Ghouls
To make their banquet relish? let me read.

'How far thro' all the bloom and brake
    That nightingale is heard!
What power but the bird's could make
    This music in the bird?
How summer-bright are yonder skies,
    And earth as fair in hue!
And yet what sign of aught that lies
    Behind the green and blue?
But man to-day is fancy's fool
    As man hath ever been.

The nameless Power, or Powers, that rule
    Were never heard or seen.'

If thou would'st hear the Nameless, and wilt dive
Into the Temple-cave of thine own self,
There, brooding by the central altar, thou
May'st haply learn the Nameless hath a voice,
By which thou wilt abide, if thou be wise,
As if thou knewest, tho' thou canst not know;
For Knowledge is the swallow on the lake
That sees and stirs the surface-shadow there
But never yet hath dipt into the abysm,
The Abysm of all Abysms, beneath, within
The blue of sky and sea, the green of earth,
And in the million-millionth of a grain
Which cleft and cleft again for evermore,
And ever vanishing, never vanishes,
To me, my son, more mystic than myself,
Or even than the Nameless is to me.
    And when thou sendest thy free soul thro'
        heaven,
Nor understandest bound nor boundlessness,
Thou seest the Nameless of the hundred names.
    And if the Nameless should withdraw from
        all
Thy frailty counts most real, all thy world
Might vanish like thy shadow in the dark.

'And since – from when this earth began –
    The Nameless never came
Among us, never spake with man,
    And never named the Name' –

Thou canst not prove the Nameless, O my son,
Nor canst thou prove the world thou movest in,
Thou canst not prove that thou art body alone,
Nor canst thou prove that thou art spirit alone,
Nor canst thou prove that thou art both in one:
Thou canst not prove thou art immortal, no
Nor yet that thou art mortal – nay my son,
Thou canst not prove that I, who speak with thee,
Am not thyself in converse with thyself,
For nothing worthy proving can be proven,
Nor yet disproven: wherefore thou be wise,
Cleave ever to the sunnier side of doubt,
And cling to Faith beyond the forms of Faith!
She reels not in the storm of warring words,
She brightens at the clash of 'Yes' and 'No,'
She sees the Best that glimmers thro' the Worst,
She feels the Sun is hid but for a night,
She spies the summer thro' the winter bud,
She tastes the fruit before the blossom falls,
She hears the lark within the songless egg,
She finds the fountain where they wail'd 'Mirage'!

> 'What Power? aught akin to Mind,
>   The mind in me and you?
> Or power as of the Gods gone blind
>   Who see not what they do?'

But some in yonder city hold, my son,
That none but Gods could build this house of ours,
So beautiful, vast, various, so beyond
All work of man, yet, like all work of man,
A beauty with defect – till That which knows,

And is not known, but felt thro' what we feel
Within ourselves is highest, shall descend
On this half-deed, and shape it at the last
According to the Highest in the Highest.

'What Power but the Years that make
    And break the vase of clay,
And stir the sleeping earth, and wake
    The bloom that fades away?
What rulers but the Days and Hours
    That cancel weal with woe,
And wind the front of youth with flowers,
    And cap our age with snow?'

    The days and hours are ever glancing by,
And seem to flicker past thro' sun and shade,
Or short, or long, as Pleasure leads, or Pain;
But with the Nameless is nor Day nor Hour;
Tho' we, thin minds, who creep from thought to thought,
Break into 'Thens' and 'Whens' the Eternal Now
This double seeming of the single world! —
My words are like the babblings in a dream
Of nightmare, when the babblings break the dream.
But thou be wise in this dream-world of ours,
Nor take thy dial for thy deity,
But make the passing shadow serve thy will.

'The years that made the stripling wise
    Undo their work again,
And leave him, blind of heart and eyes,
    The last and least of men;
Who clings to earth, and once would dare

    Hell-heat or Arctic cold,
And now one breath of cooler air
    Would loose him from his hold;
His winter chills him to the root,
    He withers marrow and mind;
The kernel of the shrivell'd fruit
    Is jutting thro' the rind;
The tiger spasms tear his chest,
    The palsy wags his head;
The wife, the sons, who love him best
    Would fain that he were dead;
The griefs by which he once was wrung
    Were never worth the while' –

Who knows? or whether this earth-narrow life
Be yet but yolk, and forming in the shell?

'The shaft of scorn that once had stung
    But wakes a dotard smile.'

The placid gleams of sunset after storm!

'The statesman's brain that sway'd the past
    Is feebler than his knees;
The passive sailor wrecks at last
    In ever-silent seas;
The warrior hath forgot his arms,
    The Learned all his lore;
The changing market frets or charms
    The merchant's hope no more;
The prophet's beacon burn'd in vain,
    And now is lost in cloud;

The plowman passes, bent with pain,
    To mix with what he plow'd;
The poet whom his Age would quote
    As heir of endless fame —
He knows not ev'n the book he wrote,
    Not even his own name.
For man has overlived his day,
    And, darkening in the light,
Scarce feels the senses break away
    To mix with ancient Night.'

The shell must break before the bird can fly.

'The years that when my Youth began
    Had set the lily and rose
By all my ways where'er they ran,
    Have ended mortal foes;
My rose of love for ever gone,
    My lily of truth and trust —
They made her lily and rose in one,
    And changed her into dust.
O rosetree planted in my grief,
    And growing, on her tomb,
Her dust is greening in your leaf,
    Her blood is in your bloom.
O slender lily waving there,
    And laughing back the light,
In vain you tell me 'Earth is fair'
    When all is dark as night.'

My son, the world is dark with griefs and graves,
So dark that men cry out against the Heavens.
Who knows but that the darkness is in man?

The doors of Night may be the gates of Light;
For wert thou born or blind or deaf, and then
Suddenly heal'd, how would'st thou glory in all
The splendours and the voices of the world!
And we, the poor earth's dying race, and yet
No phantoms, watching from a phantom shore
Await the last and largest sense to make
The phantom walls of this illusion fade,
And show us that the world is wholly fair.

> 'But vain the tears for darken'd years
>   As laughter over wine,
> And vain the laughter as the tears,
>   O brother, mine or thine,
> For all that laugh, and all that weep
>   And all that breathe are one
> Slight ripple on the boundless deep
>   That moves, and all is gone.'

But that one ripple on the boundless deep
Feels that the deep is boundless, and itself
For ever changing form, but evermore
One with the boundless motion of the deep.

> 'Yet wine and laughter friends! and set
>   The lamps alight, and call
> For golden music, and forget
>   The darkness of the pall.'

If utter darkness closed the day, my son –
But earth's dark forehead flings athwart the heavens
Her shadow crown'd with stars – and yonder – out

To northward — some that never set, but pass
From sight and night to lose themselves in day.
I hate the black negation of the bier,
And wish the dead, as happier than ourselves
And higher, having climb'd one step beyond
Our village miseries, might be borne in white
To burial or to burning, hymn'd from hence
With songs in praise of death, and crown'd with flowers!

>'O worms and maggots of to-day
>   Without their hope of wings!'

But louder than thy rhyme the silent Word
Of that world-prophet in the heart of man.

>'Tho' some have gleams or so they say
>   Of more than mortal things.'

To-day? but what of yesterday? for oft
On me, when boy, there came what then I call'd,
Who knew no books and no philosophies,
In my boy-phrase 'The Passion of the Past.'
The first gray streak of earliest summer-dawn,
The last long stripe of waning crimson gloom,
As if the late and early were but one —
A height, a broken grange, a grove, a flower
Had murmurs 'Lost and gone and lost and gone!'
A breath, a whisper — some divine farewell —
Desolate sweetness — far and far away —
What had he loved, what had he lost, the boy?
I know not and I speak of what has been.
And more, my son! for more than once when I

Sat all alone, revolving in myself
The word that is the symbol of myself,
The mortal limit of the Self was loosed,
And past into the Nameless, as a cloud
Melts into Heaven. I touch'd my limbs, the limbs
Were strange not mine – and yet no shade of doubt,
But utter clearness, and thro' loss of Self
The gain of such large life as match'd with ours
Were Sun to spark – unshadowable in words,
Themselves but shadows of a shadow-world.

    'And idle gleams will come and go,
      But still the clouds remain;'

The clouds themselves are children of the Sun.

    'And Night and Shadow rule below
      When only Day should reign.'

And Day and Night are children of the Sun,
And idle gleams to thee are light to me.
Some say, the Light was father of the Night,
And some, the Night was father of the Light,
No night no day! – I touch thy world again –
No ill no good! such counter-terms, my son,
Are border-races, holding, each its own
By endless war: but night enough is there
In yon dark city: get thee back: and since
The key to that weird casket, which for thee
But holds a skull, is neither thine nor mine,
But in the hand of what is more than man,
Or in man's hand when man is more than man,

Let be thy wail and help thy fellow men,
And make thy gold thy vassal not thy king,
And fling free alms into the beggar's bowl,
And send the day into the darken'd heart;
Nor list for guerdon in the voice of men,
A dying echo from a falling wall;
Nor care — for Hunger hath the Evil eye —
To vex the noon with fiery gems, or fold
Thy presence in the silk of sumptuous looms;
Nor roll thy viands on a luscious tongue,
Nor drown thyself with flies in honied wine;
Nor thou be rageful, like a handled bee,
And lose thy life by usage of thy sting;
Nor harm an adder thro' the lust for harm,
Nor make a snail's horn shrink for wantonness;
And more — think well! Do-well will follow thought,
And in the fatal sequence of this world
An evil thought may soil thy children's blood;
But curb the beast would cast thee in the mire,
And leave the hot swamp of voluptuousness
A cloud between the Nameless and thyself,
And lay thine uphill shoulder to the wheel,
And climb the Mount of Blessing, whence, if thou
Look higher, then — perchance — thou mayest — beyond
A hundred ever-rising mountain lines,
And past the range of Night and Shadow — see
The high-heaven dawn of more than mortal day
Strike on the Mount of Vision!
     So, farewell.

Crossing the Bar

Sunset and evening star,
    And one clear call for me!
And may there be no moaning of the bar,
    When I put out to sea,

But such a tide as moving seems asleep,
    Too full for sound and foam,
When that which drew from out the boundless deep
    Turns again home.

Twilight and evening bell,
    And after that the dark!
And may there be no sadness of farewell,
    When I embark;

For tho' from out our bourne of Time and Place
    The flood may bear me far,
I hope to see my Pilot face to face
    When I have crost the bar.

Index of First Lines

A still small voice spake unto me 87
A thousand summers ere the time of Christ 209
All along the valley, stream that flashest white 183
Altho' I be the basest of mankind 76
Ask me no more: the moon may draw the sea 157

Below the thunders of the upper deep 36
Break, break, break 117
Bury the Great Duke 162

Come into the garden, Maud 175
Comrades, leave me here a little, while as yet 'tis early morn 120
'Courage!' he said, and pointed toward the land 69

Deep on the convent-roof the snows 118
Dosn't thou 'ear my 'erse's legs, as they canters awaäy? 188

Half a league, half a league 172
He clasps the crag with crooked hands 161

I built my soul a lordly pleasure-house 53
I envy not in any moods 160
I had a vision when the night was late 144
I read, before my eyelids dropt their shade 41
I stood upon the Mountain which o'erlooks 19
I waited for the train at Coventry 141
I wish I were as in the years of old 203
It little profits that an idle king 84

Lady Clara Vere de Vere 153
Light, so low upon earth 202

Lucilia, wedded to Lucretius, found   192
On either side the river lie   134

Ring out, wild bells, to the wild sky   158

So all day long the noise of battle roll'd   107
Sunset and evening star   219

'Tears, idle tears, I know not what they mean   156
The woods decay, the woods decay and fall   179
There is a sound of thunder afar   178
There is sweet music here that softer falls   71
There lies a vale in Ida, lovelier   9
Turn, Fortune, turn thy wheel, and lower the proud   182

Wheer 'asta beän saw long and meä liggin' 'ere aloän?   184
When the breeze of a joyful dawn blew free   30
Where Claribel low-lieth   37
Who would be   28
With blackest moss the flower-plots   38
With one black shadow at its feet   65